CREATING A BEAUTIFUL MESS

Other Redleaf Press Books by Ann Gadzikowski

Challenging Exceptionally Bright Children in Early Childhood Classrooms

Story Dictation: A Guide for Early Childhood Professionals

CREATING A BEAUTIFUL MESS

Ten Essential Play Experiences for a Joyous Childhood

Ann Gadzikowski

Redleaf Press®
www.redleafpress.org
800-423-8309

Published by Redleaf Press
10 Yorkton Court
St. Paul, MN 55117
www.redleafpress.org

First edition 2015
Cover design by Elizabeth MacKinney, Berry Graphics
Interior design by Erin Kirk New
Typeset in Scala
Printed in the United States of America
22 21 20 19 18 17 16 15   1 2 3 4 5 6 7 8
Library of Congress Cataloging-in-Publication Data
Gadzikowski, Ann.
  Creating a beautiful mess : ten essential play experiences for a
joyous childhood / Ann Gadzikowski.
     pages cm
  Includes bibliographical references.
  ISBN 978-1-60554-386-4 (paperback)
1. Parenting. 2. Families. I. Title.
  HQ755.8.G323 2015
  306.874—dc23
                              2014047334

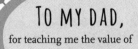

To my dad,
for teaching me the value of
a good knock-knock joke

CONTENTS

Acknowledgments

Thank you to all my beautifully messy playmates, past, present, and future. Many of the ideas expressed in this book were inspired by happy memories of my own childhood playing with my brothers, my parents, my grandma, my neighbors and friends. Later, when I was a student of child development at the Erikson Institute, Professor Lorraine Wallach first introduced me to the academic study of play. I'm grateful to Lorraine and all the other mentors and teachers who have guided my work. A special thank-you to my friend Damian Hughes for serving as my board games consultant.

I also owe many thanks to the children, families, and teachers I've worked with over the years in early childhood programs. I'm especially grateful to the parents of students in Northwestern University's CTD Leapfrog program; the questions you asked about play inspired this book.

Many thanks to all my Cleveland Street neighbors. Watching our kids play Ghost in the Graveyard at block parties convinced me that play is still play, even in the twenty-first century.

And I'm grateful for the support, encouragement, and expertise of my Redleaf team, Kyra Ostendorf, Danny Miller, and Alyssa Lochner.

But most of all, I want to thank my very favorite playmate, my daughter, Alexa. All the best fun began with you.

CREATING A BEAUTIFUL MESS

INTRODUCTION • PLAY IS STILL PLAY

Most books about this topic start with an argument in defense of play—a litany of reasons we should all value play as a legitimate use of children's time and energy. I choose instead to begin this book on the offense, ready to score, prepared to rack up an easy victory on behalf of Team Play. I can do this because the strongest evidence for the value of play already lives in you, in your heart and mind, fueled by all the positive memories of play from your own childhood. Remember that time you lay in the grass and rolled down a hill, the sky spinning over your head, the smell of wet mulch in your nose, laughing out loud when you crashed into your best friend at the bottom of the hill? Or that time you built a castle out of a cardboard box, with a maze of rooms and corridors inhabited by wizards and elves? Remember when you cuddled that beloved soft, stuffed bear, surrounded by a fort of pillows and cushions, whispering secrets in your bear's fuzzy ear? You may not have these exact memories of these exact play experiences, but you probably remember something very similar.

We each have our own direct experience with the excitement and pleasures of play. As parents, we often use our own memories of childhood play as a sort of rubric for measuring our children's experiences. In my work as a teacher and director in early childhood education for more than twenty-five years, I've listened to a lot of parents talk about play. Parents often wonder if play today is different from what they enjoyed as children. They sometimes don't recognize play in their children's behavior, especially when children use toys and materials, such as iPads, that they never had. Many parents wonder if technology has a negative effect on their children's growth and development. Most of all, parents just want to know if their children are normal, happy, and healthy.

1

The good news is that play is still play. It may look a little different, but it really hasn't changed. In this book I will remind you of the play you experienced as a child and show you the connections between those memories and the play your child is experiencing today. Some of the toys and the vocabulary of play are a bit different, but the essential play experiences are timeless.

What Is Play?

Let's take a moment to define play and ground our conversation in a shared understanding of the experience of play in the lives of children. I prefer a broad and generous definition. Play is pretty much any activity that is done purely for pleasure. While some people may find pleasure in their work, or even in chores such as washing the dishes, that's not really play, because in play, pleasure is the primary and often sole reason for doing it. Play is just for fun.

Play is pretty much any activity that is done purely for pleasure.

Play is often, but not always, something children do. But sometimes adults can play, especially when the adults are parents playing with their children. Play often, but not always, involves toys. In truth, toys are not necessary for play. The pleasure of play usually comes from freedom and spontaneity, a lack of goals or structure. When we "play with" something, it usually means we are not trying to accomplish a specific goal; we're just experimenting and seeing what happens. Play can be joyous. Children often smile and laugh when they play. But play can also be absorbing. Instead of smiles, children's faces may instead show great concentration and focus while they play. Focused, intense play is still play.

The Ten Essential Play Experiences

This book grew from my talking with parents about their children and listening to parents' questions about their children's behavior and development. I've noticed that most parents already have a good understanding of what play is and how their children benefit from it. The concerns I hear from parents have to do with balance. Most parents wonder how to balance their own family and work lives, and they are also concerned with how to find the balance between their children's free, unstructured time at home with planned activities outside the home such as music lessons and organized sports. Also, many parents wonder if their children are spending too much time involved with technology—whether it's playing computer games, watching television, or using an iPad.

My concern is less about what children are doing and more about what they're not doing. When discussing how children should be spending their time, I try to help families refocus on the goal of living balanced lives. Children benefit from exposure to a broad variety of experiences. If they are spending most of their free time doing one thing, that's probably not a good idea. So when I'm asked, "Is my child doing too much [fill in the blank]?" I like to reframe the question and ask, "Is there anything missing from your child's life? Is your child enjoying a full range of play experiences?" This concept of balance in children's play experiences is similar to the concept of nutritional balance. Suppose I drop by your house one random day and find you eating a bowl of cereal and you ask me, "Do you think I eat too much cereal?" I won't know the answer to that question unless I ask about what else you usually eat. Serving a balanced diet of play to your child follows the same pattern. If you're wondering whether your child spends too much time on the computer, or too much time playing alone with dolls, or too much time building with Lego bricks, then you need to look at what other play experiences your child is having. Is there variety? Is there balance?

The ten essential play experiences described in this book represent a full range of play experiences for a balanced and joyous childhood. There are many different ways we might categorize play into ten experiences. Early childhood educators think of play in terms of the domains of development—physical, social, emotional, cognitive, and language. Parents often think of play in terms of when and where it takes place—after school or before bed, indoors or outdoors; or perhaps in terms of how the play affects the rest of the family—quiet play or loud play. For the purposes of this book, I tried to put myself in young children's shoes and create categories of play that represent their perspectives. When children think about play, they probably think in terms of actions—for example, running, building, and laughing. This is how I organized the ten play experiences. They are not in any particular order—all are equally important—but the first six categories focus more on young children, toddlers through kindergarteners, and the last four focus more on school-age children, ages six through twelve.

1 • Building with Blocks

Building with blocks is first on the list, not because it is the most important play experience but because it is often the most overlooked. Blocks are bulky, clunky, and noisy. They take up too much room on the bedroom floor and they take too long to put away after playing. But the truth is, blocks offer the ultimate multitasking play experience because children have everything to gain from block play—they learn about physics, math, engineering, geometry, architecture, and design. Block play develops physical skills such as dexterity and balance. And when children play together with blocks they learn to collaborate, communicate, negotiate, and connect.

Even if you take away all the amazing educational and developmental reasons for sitting your child in front of a pile of blocks, there's still the simple, pure truth that stacking one block on top of another is one of the most satisfying actions a child can do during play. What could be more pleasurable than taking one plain block and adding to it, turning it into something bigger, taller, higher in the sky with each block you add? The only action more empowering than stacking blocks into a tower is knocking down the whole stack.

Block building is not just for boys. Girls can and should be encouraged to construct their own buildings, cities, and worlds. Girls need to know that a toy doesn't have to be pink in order for a female person to play with it (more on that later).

When children create structures out of wooden blocks (or foam blocks, or Lego bricks, or, for that matter, cardboard boxes from the recycling bin), they are constructing more than buildings; they are developing and expanding their problem-solving skills and capacity for abstract thought. They are almost literally building bridges from one idea to the next. In chapter 1, we'll look closely at the cognitive, physical, and social benefits of block play and how to promote and facilitate your child's block play experiences.

2 • Pretending and Make-Believe

Pretend play seems to take place spontaneously among children of every culture across the world. In very young children it often begins when small toddlers pretend to be Mommy or Daddy, toting Mommy's purse or shuffling across the floor in Daddy's big shoes. This kind of role-playing has a practical function—it is a rehearsal for real life, the earliest iteration of "Fake it 'til you make it."

Pretend play is also a form of storytelling and fantasizing. As children's minds develop and their imaginations take hold, they progress from pretending to be a mommy or daddy to pretending to be a mermaid, pirate, superhero, or wizard. Pretend play becomes an escape, a vacation from the ordinary world, a chance to soar above everyday experience. Pretend play is also a way to interact with other children and create a deeply meaningful social connection.

Pretend play often goes by the name "make-believe." In pretend play, children "make" themselves (and each other) "believe" that a towel can be a cape, a closet can be a castle, or a little girl can be the ruler of the whole wide world. A large body of research supports the idea that pretend play and make-believe are important ingredients in children's mental health, particularly during stressful times. But pretending does not always come easily to every child. Some children need encouragement and modeling to learn how to pretend, especially now that there are computer games and mobile apps to distract children from their own stories and ideas. A parent's role in pretend play is just one of the many issues explored in chapter 2.

3 • Running Around Like Crazy

The glorious experience of running across a grassy lawn at full steam can hardly be described in words. The freedom of all-out physical exertion defies definition and can't be held inside the confines of the text on this page.

Human children, like puppies, antelopes, sharks, and cheetahs, just need to move to be alive. Physical exercise is essential for health and well-being. Pick up any newspaper or visit any news site and you'll read about the prevalence of childhood obesity, the extinction of school recess, and the diminishing green play spaces in urban areas. The experts agree: children need more opportunities to run around like crazy cakes.

This essential play experience includes other forms of physical movement, such as climbing, skipping, dancing, or rolling down a hill. In chapter 3 we'll look at ways parents can help make sure their children get out and move.

4 • Cuddling Something Soft and Small

All young children, boys as well as girls, need to find something smaller and softer than they are, something they can hold and hug and cuddle and love. Most children will find a special lovey without any assistance from an adult. It will probably be a doll or stuffed animal, but it might be something more unusual, such as a scrap of a baby blanket, one of Daddy's old T-shirts, or a dishcloth. Often the special lovey becomes a friend, a confidant, or even an extension of the child, a surrogate in times of stress ("Baby bear is scared, she needs a hug from Mommy.").

Not every child will naturally gravitate toward a special soft lovey. Some actually prefer the solid, smooth texture of plastic or rubber toys. Others may prefer to strike out into the world on their own, unencumbered by a special toy. The complex gender, cultural, and developmental issues involving cuddling soft toys will be explored in chapter 4.

5 • Laughing, Joking, and Other General Silliness

Laughter is the currency of childhood; it is more valuable than gold or silver, stocks and bonds. For many children, the first joke they make involves putting something ridiculous on top of their heads—a shoe, a handful of spaghetti, the dog's slobbery bone. What could be more delightful than a toddler with something completely silly balanced on top of his big round head, squealing with delight? From peekaboo games to wet, messy "raspberries," the young child's arsenal of funny gestures and sounds is endless. Over time, as children grow and develop, their humor becomes more sophisticated, such as the slapstick hilarity of the kids who shake up your bottle of diet soda at the family picnic or the nuanced potty talk of third-grade boys. The surprising value of humor in child development and the parent's role in encouraging this funny business will be discussed in chapter 5.

6 • Creating a Beautiful Mess

I've traveled far from my own childhood (nostalgia alert!), but when I close my eyes I can still remember the yeasty smell of fingerpaints in my kindergarten classroom. I vividly recall the smooth texture of the paints, thick as toothpaste, on the shiny paper. Back then, no one saved our paintings or posted images of them on Instagram because creating a gallery of masterpieces wasn't the point. The main thing was the process—the sensory experience of smearing that gooey mess across the page, the tips of our smock sleeves dragging over the tacky surface of the paint. Fingerpainting is much rarer today. Advancements in the technology of children's art products have provided us with "no mess" paints, markers, and clay. These days, it seems there is always a layer of clear plastic between children and their art supplies.

What's missing here? Children must make messes. It's in their job description. They must knead playdough, splash water, slap mud pies, blow bubbles. Some parents may find this news discouraging, especially if they have light-colored carpeting in the family room. There are, however, some commonsense strategies for reducing damage to your home. The valid, research-based arguments for allowing children to safely enjoy these sensory experiences will be detailed in chapter 6.

7 • Playing Turn-Taking Games

This next play experience, turn-taking games, is a close cousin to the running-around-like-crazy play experience. Most children love the thrill of the chase, of escaping or of being "it." But we often forget that the world of games is so much bigger than Tag. I believe there are two broad categories of games, those I call "playground games" and those I call "table games." Playground games include running-around games such as Tag, Kick the Can, and Ghost in the Graveyard, as well as jump rope games, ball games, hiding games, clapping games, and thumb wrestling. Table games include any kind of board game or card game or games using dice or playing pieces, including pen-and-paper guessing games.

The pleasure of playing games with other people is very different from playing on your own. It's like the difference between humming your own sweet tune and having an opportunity to play a musical instrument in an orchestra. Each activity brings very different pleasures and very different challenges. The social interactions, the turn taking, the negotiations and alliance building that go on during game playing make this a truly essential play experience. Through games, children learn to understand and follow rules, self-regulate, listen, remember, and strategize.

Also, playing games with friends and families can be hilarious. Think about the times in your life when you laughed so hard you almost peed your pants. I bet it happened when you were playing a game. Parents, however, are sometimes bored with the repetitive nature of children's games and may be reluctant to respond to their children's pleas to "Play with me!" Chapter 7 examines some of the possibilities for parents to find games they truly enjoy playing with their children. For example, we'll discuss the widespread misconception that Monopoly is a great family board game and look, instead, at the wide range of alternatives.

8 • Finding and Collecting Things

When my daughter was young, from about age two to five, every time we went for a walk in our neighborhood she would pick up at least one rock and bring it home. We collected so many rocks her room began to look like a quarry. Collecting things is a common childhood activity. Many children (and adults) enjoy collecting items that can be purchased from stores, such as Pokémon cards, comic books, or charms for a bracelet. But this essential play experience is not really about things you buy at the mall. It's about the rocks, shells, leaves, sticks, and acorns we find outdoors. It's also about the discarded treasures that captivate children's imaginations—the shiny gold candy wrapper, the pink plastic ring from the juice bottle cap, or the little milk carton that looks like a tiny house with a slanted roof.

Children enjoy finding the secrets that adults have overlooked. They love to make something out of nothing: a plastic bowl can become a boat, a handful of paper clips can be made into a necklace. Sometimes the pleasure in finding and collecting is the ability to keep adding more and more to the collection. A wealth of small items, such as buttons or bolts, can be endlessly counted, sorted, and categorized.

The process of finding and collecting interesting stuff increases our awareness of the world around us and makes us more conscientious about how we use our resources. A collection can be a group of items or objects in a box, but a collection can also be a group of experiences, such as keeping a list of the cars you see with out-of-state license plates. The pleasure is in the pursuit and discovery. Chapter 8 examines the ways parents can support and encourage their children in the finding and collecting of interesting stuff. Sometimes it's as simple as giving your child a box to put her rocks in.

9 • Telling Stories with Toys

Every culture has stories to tell. Stories offer a way of collecting, remembering, and honoring our experiences. Children sense this in the ways their ears prick up each time they hear "Once upon a time . . ." Telling a story is serious business but it is also part of play. Children tell stories with words and actions, through pretend play with toys and props, or they tell stories without words, through drawings or sound effects and movement as they play with Spider-Man figures or Polly Pocket Playsets.

If there were a family tree of essential play experiences, telling a story with toys would be closely related to pretending and make-believe. Both play experiences stretch the imagination. Chapter 9 looks at the complexity of storytelling in the lives of young children and the role of parents in nurturing that process.

I have yet to meet a child who did not enjoy pushing buttons in an elevator. In child development circles, the concept is called "cause and effect." Children want to shake things up and make things happen. They figure out very quickly that buttons, machines, and technology are the way to go. By "machines" I mean all machines: simple nonmotorized machines such as bikes, machines with ordinary motors such as remote-control toy trucks and cars, and machines with computer chips and screens—sophisticated computers and other electronic devices, such as iPads and cell phones.

I use the word "machines" here because so many parents are terrified of "technology." We are afraid of all these devices that we love to use but don't fully understand, the devices that are going to take over our children's minds and turn them into robotic zombies. In chapter 10, I'll remind you that you are in control of what happens in your home and can make reasoned and informed choices about what machines your children play with. From children's perspective, the appeal of playing with machines is not going away anytime soon. We just need to make sure they're pushing the right buttons.

Learning How to Play

One of my favorite quotes from pediatrician and author T. Berry Brazelton is, "Parents need to understand that they can relax and have fun, because the baby will teach them how to become a parent" (NPR 2013). I so agree. Parents, your children will teach you how to play, a process that will bring you great joy.

Ready?

Set.

Go!

Building with Blocks

Twins Chloe and Zoe are building a city on their bedroom floor. They begin by each hoarding her favorite blocks. Chloe likes the rare, curved shapes—the arches and round pillars. Zoe, however, wants all the rectangles, the uniform brick shapes—she knows these are valuable because they will be needed to form the strongest walls.

Like wise urban planners, the girls first create the roads. Then they begin building houses, dog parks, and ice cream parlors. Their mother looks in on the girls from time to time, but the children are so absorbed in their tasks that they hardly speak or look up as they play. When the pile of available blocks in the shared bin runs low, they negotiate with each other for the remaining shapes in their individual reserves. Chloe needs two more rectangles to put a roof on the puppy café. Zoe needs a curved arch for the gateway to the butterfly hospital. An exchange is made and the city is complete.

Once the last block is in place, the sisters immediately abandon the project and move to the dining table to draw. Their mother, however, stands in the doorway of the bedroom, admiring the city her daughters have constructed. They've used every block in the two-hundred-piece set and have created a complex landscape of towers, structures, enclosures, ramped streets, fences, and gates. She asks the girls, "You worked for more than an hour creating this amazing city—don't you want to play with it now?" Chloe responds with a blank stare. Already absorbed in her new task, Zoe doesn't even look up from her drawing. At age four, the girls don't yet have the vocabulary to explain to their mother that with block play, often the construction process is more satisfying than using the completed structures in pretend play.

"Well, if you're finished playing with the blocks, then you need to clean them up."

This gets their attention. Both girls turn to their mother and wail, "No!"

Chloe and Zoe's mother is a smart woman and she knows how to pick her battles. She sees that the girls are already engaged in coloring, so she resolves to make them clean up the blocks as soon as they finish with their drawings. But life gets in the way again, as it often does, and the twins' mother forgets about the blocks until after dinner, when the family is clearing the table and Zoe fishes a plastic strawberry basket out of the recycling bin.

"Mommy, can I have this?" she asks.

"Hmm, I guess so," her mother replies. "Let's rinse it off first and make sure it's clean. Why do you want it?"

Chloe replies, "She wants it for the pet store, right, Zoe?"

"Right," says Zoe as she rinses the little green basket. "It's for keeping the snakes from eating the birds." Zoe dries the basket and carries it into the bedroom. Her mother watches as the girls make small additions and adjustments to the block city they constructed earlier in the day. She doesn't have the heart to make them put away the blocks now, not after seeing how the girls' ideas have continued to percolate and grow over the course of the day.

"Would you like to keep the blocks out overnight, and save your city until tomorrow?" she asks her daughters. Both girls answer with huge smiles.

The Pleasures of Block Play

Pick up a wooden block and feel the heft of the wood in your hand. Run your fingers along the sanded surface. Smell it. Go ahead, take a good sniff, and you might detect a faint aroma of pine or sawdust. Now take two blocks and carefully stack one on top of the other. Did you hear that? There was a muted tap when one flat wood surface met another. Now do it again. Place one block on another, but this time, let gravity do the work for you. Let the top block fall onto the bottom block. Now what did you hear? A louder, more percussive sound: a slap.

Whether your blocks are made of wood, plastic, foam, or cardboard, playing with them engages so many of our senses—touch, sight, smell, and hearing. The complex sensory experience of block play is just one of the reasons why children gain so much from the experience of block play. The way we move our bodies during block play is almost athletic. We lift and reach; we move our hands and fingers with grace and dexterity as we balance roofs on walls and peaks on towers. Many children and adults find block play to be visually very satisfying. We enjoy the symmetry and balance of our constructions, the ways the smooth edges fit together, how the light creates shadows in the gaps between structures.

Much of the pleasure of block play comes from the opportunities to make glorious and terrible mistakes with little consequence. Watch a child build with blocks and you'll notice that if the child is fully engaged and active, her structures will fall down at least half the time. But good, solid toy blocks rarely break. We just pick them up and try again. The trial and error inherent in block play is one of the reasons children learn so much from the experience. They learn science concepts involved in structural engineering, but they also develop the ability to solve problems through failure. Children who play with blocks develop the muscle memory for moving through mistakes and finding success.

> *Much of the pleasure of block play comes from the opportunities to make glorious and terrible mistakes.*

Another significant pleasure of playing with blocks comes from the satisfaction of making something really, really big. Who wants to play with just a tiny handful of little baby blocks? We want lots and lots of blocks and we want big blocks, blocks the size of real bricks, blocks bigger than your head, blocks that can be stacked all the way up to the ceiling, or maybe even to the moon! What begins as the pure pleasure of placing one block on top of the other, when infused with a bit of creative imagination, takes flight and becomes something extraordinary.

Block play inspires all kinds of imaginative play and creative thought. When I was a little girl, my brothers and I played with a large set of wooden blocks in a basement playroom. It was an area of the house just beyond the laundry room that was rarely used by adults, which meant we didn't have to clean up the blocks very often. We were able to spread out and create large structures and landscapes. Oddly, one of my most vivid childhood memories involving blocks is of a structure I never actually saw with my own eyes. When I was about seven years old, one of my older brothers got in trouble for something he did with the blocks in the basement. I came home from school and found he had been sent to his room, but no one would tell me why. That evening, over dinner, I could tell by the stern look on my mother's face that my brother must have done something really, really bad. Later, I learned that he and his friend had built a city of blocks in the basement and had decided it would be fun to use real candles to light the city. They took from the kitchen a package of birthday candles that came with little candleholders and propped up the candles at strategic positions around their city. Somehow they also got their hands on a package of matches. They lit the candles, turned off the lights, and enjoyed the view of their block city illuminated by candlelight. My mother discovered them and, of course, she was furious. The friend was immediately sent home and my brother was banished to his bedroom.

As a child, I was both horrified and fascinated by this story. Later, during block play, whenever I came across a block still stained with a bit of candle wax, I would try to imagine that illuminated city of blocks. The danger and daring of using real matches to light real candles among wooden blocks contributed to my excitement about and fascination with the story. But what really captured my imagination, and still lingers in my mind today, is that image of the illuminated block city, magical in the flickering light of the flames. I'm aware that today a similar effect could be safely created using battery-operated tea lights, but I prefer to continue to let the candles burn in my imagination. For you and your child, however, I recommend the safe tea lights! Build the city, place the lights at the tops of the towers and along the street corners. Then turn the lights off and let the magic begin.

The Benefits of Block Play

Young children have been stacking pieces of stone, wood, and bricks since the dawn of time, but the concept of blocks of uniform size as a construction toy goes back to German educator Friedrich Froebel in the early nineteenth century. Froebel has come to be known as "the father of kindergarten" because he was one of the first educators to develop a learning curriculum for very young children. His term "Kindergarten," still in use today, means "children's garden," and Froebel believed that a child's learning can grow, as a flower grows in a garden, nurtured through play and conversation, gently guided by teachers. Among Froebel's most enduring ideas was the significance of block play. Froebel designed classroom toys that he called "gifts," a number of which are still in use in some schools today. Each gift is a set of toys that children manipulate, and the progression from one gift to the next is designed to increase in complexity and present greater and greater challenges to the child's mind. The very first gift, Froebel Gift 1, for example, is a set of simple balls made of yarn. Children hold, squeeze, roll, and throw the balls as a playful introduction to shape, dimension, and the physics of motion. Most of the Froebel gifts, however, are sets of wooden blocks. For example, Froebel Gift 3 consists of eight small cubes and Gift 4 consists of eight small oblong bricklike blocks. The architect Frank Lloyd Wright frequently credited the Froebel blocks from his childhood as a significant influence on his understanding of architecture (Rubin 1989). In reference to his experience building with Froebel blocks, Wright is frequently quoted as saying, "The maple wood blocks . . . are in my fingers to this day" (Guggenheim Foundation 2014). That kinesthetic memory of having the blocks "in my fingers" is something I've observed in the play experiences of preschool children. Ask a child at the lunch table what she built in the block corner that morning, and she is likely to put down her fork and move her hands as she talks, placing imaginary blocks on her plate as she describes the house or tower she built.

The blocks I played with as a child—still commonly in use today—are called "unit blocks." An American educator, Caroline Pratt, developed the design of unit blocks in the early twentieth century. Pratt was very much influenced by Froebel in the design of unit blocks, but Pratt wanted children to have a larger, broader, more open-ended play experience with blocks (Hirsch 1996). While Froebel blocks are small, intended for use on a table or desk, the basic brick or "unit" in Pratt's blocks is more than four times the size of a Froebel brick. Unit blocks are best used on the floor, where children can spread out, play with friends, and create large structures.

The basic unit, or brick, in standard unit blocks is 5.5 inches long, 2.75 inches wide, and 1.375 inches thick. All the other shapes in the set are standardized sizes and ratios in relation to the unit. For example, two square blocks equal one unit. Two units equal one long oblong block. This standardization of sizes and ratios creates opportunities for children to discover and explore mathematical and scientific concepts, a kinesthetic introduction to geometry and engineering. For example, children who play with blocks, such as the twins Chloe and Zoe in our opening scenario, develop an understanding of which shapes create the most stable foundation for their buildings. Through block play the girls learn that a house built with rectangular bricks, or units, is far more stable than a house built with just squares. The rectangular bricks provide more surface and weight for stability, whereas the squares, with each side of equal length, tend to slip when bumped.

Wooden unit blocks are available for purchase from most toy retailers. Although the best-quality sets are made from the heaviest woods, maple or birch, sets made of less expensive woods, such as beech or rubber wood, are perfectly fine. Traditional unit blocks are sanded but not finished with varnish or paint. Sets of unit blocks usually range in price from $50 to $300. The size of each set can vary too, usually starting at one hundred blocks. When several children are playing together with blocks, I recommend having at least two hundred blocks available, to avoid conflicts while providing enough raw material for really exciting structures.

How Block Play Develops

Of course, the first time a young child plays with blocks, she won't be able to immediately build a model of the Taj Mahal. Just as most children learn to crawl before they walk, most children, when first exposed to blocks, will begin holding and carrying them, perhaps hugging them or throwing them, as they initially explore their properties. Harriet Merrill Johnson, a colleague of Caroline Pratt, the creator of unit blocks, observed children's block play and proposed a developmental sequence of behaviors that all or most children seem to follow as they learn about blocks and begin enjoying block play. Johnson proposed the following seven stages of block play (Johnson 1966).

Stage 1: Carrying

Age two is an appropriate time to introduce children to blocks because they have developed the ability to grasp, hold, and move toys. At this young age, however, most children are not yet able to build structures. Toddlers and two-year-olds are more likely to enjoy carrying blocks in their hands or collecting blocks in a bag or basket. Children usually very much enjoy dumping a pile of blocks onto the floor, especially if the blocks make a very loud noise. This is how children get to know the properties of blocks: the texture, weight, smell, sound, and, sometimes, for children who still like to suck on or lick their toys, the taste. At this stage, parents and caregivers may need to wash the blocks periodically in mild soapy water. (Many children enjoy helping with that task.)

Stage 2: Building

Around age three, most children will begin building very simple structures with blocks. They will stack the blocks either vertically, in a tower, or horizontally, in a road. This is the stage when children really begin to learn the physics of blocks. Through trial and error they discover, for example, that a big block stacked on a small block often falls, but when the big block is placed first, as a foundation, the smaller block rests solidly on top. Children derive a great deal of satisfaction from stacking blocks, but if an adult asks, "What are you making?," children often respond with a blank stare. They are building for the sake of building, enjoying the process more than the result, and, at this stage, children usually have not thought about what their structures will be or what they represent.

Stage 3: Bridging

When a child places two blocks side by side in parallel positions, with space between, and adds another block on top, the bridgelike structure she creates is the next step in developing greater complexity and sophistication in block play. This bridging stage often develops around age three or four, depending on how much experience the child has had building with blocks. Children often don't name their structures "bridges." And they frequently learn to create these bridgelike structures by imitating the older children or adults who play with them.

Stage 4: Enclosing

Four-year-olds often create enclosures consisting of rows of blocks placed like walls or fences around toy cars or animals. Often children build a wall around themselves, like a fort. This common behavior of young children during block play represents a growing awareness of the different kinds of structures that can be created using blocks. The process of creating enclosures offers interesting problems to solve, for example, how to build around obstacles such as furniture or other children. Building enclosures also challenges children to begin thinking about the design of entrances and exits: how will the animals get in and out of their enclosure?

Stage 5: Making Decorative Patterns

Around ages four and five, children begin to take pleasure in creating patterns and symmetry with blocks. Instead of building a tower or enclosure, a child may prefer to collect all the triangle blocks and lay them in a pattern across the rug, creating a zigzag of pointed shapes. Although they usually don't yet know the meaning of the word "symmetry," at this stage in development, children begin to pay more attention to the aesthetics of the structures they create, taking care to balance the placement of blocks on each side, often creating mirrored symmetry in their block creations.

Stage 6: Naming

At some point around age four, children become much more deliberate and organized in their block play. They begin planning ahead of time what they might build ("I'm going to make a house for the dinosaurs."). At this stage, they are also more able to collaborate with other children in building something together because they are developing the language to talk about what they want to make ("You find some triangles to make the roof."). Now, when an adult asks "What did you make?," children often have an elaborate answer.

Stage 7: Symbolizing

The more experience children have with blocks, the more complex, developed, and sophisticated their creations will be. The final stage of block play, symbolizing, begins around age five and will last through the rest of childhood. By this stage, children have developed enough capacity for abstract thought that they can imagine how their structure made of blocks represents or symbolizes something that might exist in the real world or the world of their imagination. Using blocks, children might build a model of their own house, or a famous landmark such as the Eiffel Tower. Or they might create a structure from their own imagination, such as a magic castle for flying elephants. The twin block builders, Chloe and Zoe, are at this stage in the development of their block play. Not only are they able to create a complex structure with multiple parts and functions, they also are able to reflect upon what they have built and make additions and improvements.

Learning through Block Play

Whenever I talk about block play with friends and colleagues, someone will inevitably bring up the topic of Legos. Playing with plastic Lego bricks offers many of the same challenges and opportunities for problem solving that children experience when playing with wooden blocks. You might think that blocks are easier to build with, since they are larger than Legos, but remember that blocks don't link together. Stacking wooden blocks means placing one smooth surface against another. When children play with wooden blocks they must utilize motor skills, hand-eye coordination, and patience in order to create a balanced and strong structure. I would argue that children learn more about physics, engineering, and construction through block play than they do through Lego play. Also, the ratios of size and proportion in wooden unit blocks demonstrate mathematic concepts of fractions and division, as well as geometric concepts of area, perimeter, and angles. Playing with wooden blocks allows children to feel the weight and texture of the blocks' various shapes and sizes, providing a multisensory experience that plastic toys can't offer.

All construction play has value, regardless of which type of toy or materials children use, especially when children are collaborating and communicating with others in the process. Opportunities for planning, problem solving, and negotiating are available whenever children play, but this is especially true when children are building something together or with their parents or caregivers. Communication during block play can include statements of leadership ("Let's build a fort!"), questions ("Where should we put the lookout tower?"), assertions ("The gate is too small. Let's make it wider."), and even humor ("Let's call it Fort Poop!"). Building and developing communication skills are another reason children grow and learn through block play.

Why Are Blocks Disappearing?

Although blocks provide such a rich and creative experience, most children today have fewer opportunities to play with blocks than their parents did. A set of wooden unit blocks was once standard equipment in American kindergarten classrooms. But, unfortunately, blocks have disappeared from most kindergartens and even from many preschool classrooms. Even back in the 1990s, when I was a student teacher in a public elementary school, only one of the three kindergarten classrooms in the school still had a shelf of blocks available to the children. I recall how the teacher in that classroom sighed and shook her head when I asked about the prevalence of block play in kindergarten. Now, in the twenty-first century, blocks are the dinosaurs of early childhood education, extinct relics of an ancient age. Researchers of trends in education confirm this conclusion: blocks are no longer part of kindergarten classrooms. "The traditional kindergarten classroom that most adults remember from childhood—with plenty of space and time for unstructured play and discovery, art and music, practicing social skills, and learning to enjoy learning—has largely disappeared" (Miller and Almon 2009, 11).

In schools, block play has often been replaced by two-dimensional "Learn Your Shapes" worksheets. At home, block play has been replaced with virtual block games like Minecraft. Actual block play, however, differs significantly from virtual block play. The tactile and sensory experience of playing with real blocks offers a deeper and more satisfying learning experience than working with shapes and figures on a page or on a screen.

 Playing with real blocks offers a deeper learning experience than shapes and figures on a screen.

Gaining opportunities to play with blocks may be especially crucial to young girls. Blocks are often perceived by both adults and children as toys for boys. Even in my own experience as a child, with a generous supply of blocks in my basement, I always knew the blocks belonged to my brothers, not to me. Debbie Sterling, engineer and designer of GoldieBlox toys, asserts that without girls' exposure to challenging construction toys, women will continue to be underrepresented in STEM (science, technology, engineering, and math) fields of study and careers (Burnett 2013). Block play is a way to even the playing field for both genders.

Block Play at Home

Building with blocks is an essential play experience. Block play is satisfying and fun. It teaches children about the world and how the pieces of the world fit together. Every child should have the opportunity to create structures out of open-ended materials such as wooden unit blocks. Through block play, children may develop a particular interest or talent in construction, architecture, geometry, or engineering. Girls must have as many opportunities to play with blocks as boys do.

Parents determine how and when children play with blocks. If there are no blocks at school or if the opportunities to play with blocks at school are limited, parents should make an effort to have blocks available at home.

This is not always easy. The primary obstacles to block play at home are cost and space. In terms of cost, it's true that a large set of wooden unit blocks may cost significantly more than plastic or foam blocks, but if a family is able to make the purchase, it's an investment in years of constructive, creative play. If you could calculate the cost of a toy by the number of hours your child plays with that toy over an entire childhood, unit blocks would show themselves to be a sound investment. But there are certainly less expensive wooden blocks available to families. When my daughter was very small, we bought her a set of small wooden blocks, similar to unit blocks but about half the size in scale, for around $40. She played with those blocks almost every day for about four years. So that $40 set of blocks cost us about $10 a year, or about three cents a day. I admit we never invested in a full set of unit blocks at home, partly because my daughter's preschool provided daily opportunities for extended block play, and partly because our apartment was fairly small.

Lack of space, for storage and for play, is another obstacle to block play at home, because a full set of unit blocks, stored in a box or a bin or stacked on a shelf, does take up a fair amount of space. Playing with unit blocks at home requires a fair amount of floor space, too, the equivalent area of a five-by-eight-foot rug. But the benefits of block play are worth the effort. Try to find a place for blocks in your budget and in your home.

What Kinds of Blocks Should Be Used at Home?

Wood is by far the best material for blocks. Plastic or foam blocks are available, especially for very young children, but plastic or foam is not as heavy as wood. A plastic or foam block doesn't give you the feel of the heft of wood in your hand, and those blocks are not as stable for building. As mentioned earlier, the sensory pleasures of building with wood include the smell and the texture of the wood. In addition to the material, also consider the variety of shapes in a set of blocks. You might think that the more variety, the better.

A set of blocks that includes curved arches and pointed spirals may appear to be exciting and creative, but make sure such a set also includes a majority of standard building shapes such as rectangles (bricks) and squares. I recently came across a set of wooden blocks in a shop. The salesperson was very pleased to explain to me that this particular set contained one block each of every shape the toy company had ever made. I decided not to tell him what a ridiculous idea that was. What can you build with one block of each shape? Not only would you lack the quantity of bricks to build any kind of foundation for your structure, but there also would be absolutely no symmetry. I'd rather have a set of all rectangles or all squares. That would be a fine set, indeed. Why doesn't anyone sell one like that?

Storage

In most early childhood classrooms, blocks are usually stored on a low, open shelf next to a rug with a low pile, not shag. Block structures should be built on a completely flat, smooth surface. While a lumpy rug might present a unique problem-solving challenge to a more advanced architect, the uneven surface will create frustration in beginning builders. A rug with a low pile is better than a tile or wood floor because the materials of the rug will help muffle the noise. Block play can be very noisy, both from the sounds of the blocks falling or bumping together and from the excited exclamations and conversations of the builders. While a bedroom or playroom might not have as much *Speaking* space as a preschool classroom, a low shelf near the floor *of putting blocks* is an ideal storage space because, unlike a bag, box, or bin, *away, don't* an open shelf allows children to see all the shapes of blocks *do it.* available. This also makes it easier and more interesting to put the blocks away, because children have the opportunity to sort and assemble the blocks on the shelf in an orderly fashion.

Speaking of putting blocks away, don't do it. Postpone putting away blocks whenever possible. As we saw in our opening scenario with Chloe and Zoe, when the children were allowed to leave their block structure intact, they discovered interesting additions and enhancements they could try later.

This concept of reusing or reconfiguring blocks as a way of deepening the play experience was part of Froebel's original vision for block play. Recall the Froebel gifts that are sets of wooden blocks—Froebel intended that when children were finished building a structure, instead of knocking it down and starting over again, they would continually change and adapt and adjust what they had already built in order to discover new ways to build. Froebel believed this process was challenging and exciting to young minds. I completely agree, but what Froebel left out of his curriculum was the plain old fun of knocking something down and creating a huge crash. There's value in the noise and drama, too.

I must mention one other way to overcome the obstacle of lack of space for blocks: take them outside! I recently visited a preschool in London and learned about an initiative among British early childhood programs to provide children with more opportunities to play outdoors. At Tachbrook Nursery School, the outdoor play space included a paved patio and several open shelves of large hollow blocks. Children could build with blocks outdoors, all year round. In addition to the blocks there were also many interesting objects and materials (e.g., wooden poles, ropes, and fabric) that could be used in combination with the blocks to create structures, tents, and forts. This experience suggests to me that a family with limited indoor space could take blocks outdoors, onto a patio or balcony, or even carry the blocks to a park in a wagon.

Supplementing blocks with other items, such as sticks and fabric, can enhance block play both indoors and out. Small toys such as cars and trucks, or figures such as animals, dinosaurs, and people, can also enhance block play. Keep a small pad of paper, pencils, or crayons, and some tape near the play area, too, in case the need arises to add a sign or label to a block structure during play ("Beware of dragons!").

Wooden blocks can also be used in combination with other kinds of construction toys, such as Lego bricks. As mentioned earlier, plastic construction toys like Legos don't share the same characteristics and benefits of block play. Keep in mind that standard Legos are too tiny for children younger than three years old and can be a choking hazard for children who put toys in their mouths. Duplo bricks are larger versions of Legos and suitable for toddlers. Many children really enjoy playing with Duplos, Legos, and other plastic construction toys. While wooden blocks should be considered as the main part, or "entrée," of your child's experience with construction toys, many of these plastic building sets make for wonderful side dishes. In addition to Legos, other recommended construction sets that are especially suited for older children include K'NEX, Magna-Tiles, and Tinker Toys.

Connect with Your Child During Block Play

Most children really enjoy it when their parents join in their block play. You may notice that they seem more engaged and excited about block play when you are playing with them. Let your child take the lead and decide what to build and how to build it. Assist them or copy what they are doing. Ask them questions, but try to be specific rather than general. For example, "What are you building?" may be hard to answer for children who haven't yet developed the ability to plan ahead. But "Which shape do you need next?" is more specific. When making conversations during block play, even better than questions are statements and observations. "I see you're balancing the cube on top of the tower." This kind of narration lets your child know you're paying close attention and you value what she is doing. You are also modeling the use of block vocabulary, using words like "cube" and "balance" which may be new to your child.

When your child is finished with her structure, rather than simply praising her ("That's a great castle."), make statements and ask questions that help your child appreciate and understand her own accomplishments ("The castle has a very tall tower. How did you make it so tall? Was that hard to do?"). Above all, keep the tone light and fun. After all, this is play. There should be an ease and joy to block play, even when it is challenging. If you and your child build with blocks together on a regular basis, you will soon find sources of inspiration all around you. On walks in your neighborhood, point out to your child the different architectural features on the buildings and houses—the slope of a roof or the shape of a window. Later, when you play together, remind your child about these features and see if you can re-create them with blocks. Look for architecture books in the children's section of your local library and use the photos and drawings for inspiration when building block structures. Take photos of the structures your child creates and put the prints in a photo album to keep on the toy shelf near the blocks. Like Chloe and Zoe in the opening scenario, your child may soon be building vast cities with features and innovations beyond your imagination.

PRETENDING AND MAKE-BELIEVE

One flat sheet, two folding chairs, a broom, and three couch cushions.

These ordinary household items have been magically transformed into a pirate ship by four-year-old Jack and his three-year-old cousin, Rowan.

"Avast!" cries Jack, brandishing a "sword" made out of cardboard.

"A blast!" mimics Rowan, waving a crayon with a menacing grin.

"No," says Jack. "Pirates say 'avast' and stuff when they want to capture someone. I'm capturing these sailors." Jack points to a pile of stuffed animals.

"Avast! Avast!" Rowan shouts at the pile of soft toys, poking them with her foot.

"Put the prisoners below deck!" orders Jack. "Except for this one." He holds up a teddy bear. "We'll make this one walk the plank!"

Rowan grabs the pile of stuffed animals and hides them under a blanket. Jack takes a stack of picture books and lines them up in a row on the floor, creating a path leading out of the fortlike pirate ship that he and Rowan built with cushions and folding chairs.

"The plank is ready!" announces Jack.

Jack's father is sitting across the room, sipping a cup of coffee and watching Jack and Rowan play. He watches Jack place the teddy bear on the plank and poke the bear with his cardboard sword.

"Prepare to die, traitor!" Jack yells.

"Die! Die!" shouts Rowan, jumping up and down.

Jack's father stops drinking his coffee and watches the two children. He remembers how, just last night, Jack cuddled that same teddy bear in bed. And Jack's dad is surprised and a little bit horrified that his sweet little niece is taking such gleeful pleasure in the impending death of the little bear. At the same time, Jack's dad remembers playing pirates and soldiers with his brother, Rowan's dad, when he was little. They had been pretty eager to kill off their "enemies" as well.

Jack pushes the teddy bear off the edge of the book plank and onto the carpet of the ocean. Rowan presses the bear into the floor and shouts, "Eat him up! The sharks eat him up!"

Both children smile and laugh. Jack turns to the pile of stuffed animals and says, "Who's next?"

Jack's dad shakes his head and pours himself another cup of coffee.

Let's Pretend

Pretending is an essential and universal play experience. Children of every culture around the world engage in make-believe, also known as "dramatic play" or "fantasy play." Our young pirates, Jack and Rowan, are at an age when pretend play is especially ripe, between the ages of three and six. Sometimes the edges between real and pretend are distinct and observable. A pretend play session may begin with an official announcement, "Let's pretend . . ." Children may use props or costumes that demonstrate they are acting out a pretend scenario. In many early childhood classrooms an area of the room usually is set aside for pretend play and equipped with items such as a little table and chairs, a toy sink, or a stove. In classrooms, these play spaces are sometimes called "the housekeeping area" or "the house area." As a preschool teacher, I was accustomed to observing the pretending that took place in these designated areas, with designated props, and with a great deal of negotiation of roles.

"You be the mommy and I'll be the baby."

"I don't want to be the baby. I'll be the auntie."

"What about Jamie? Who can Jamie be?"

"Jamie can be the baby, but only if she doesn't cry too loud like last time."

Pretend play in early childhood classrooms is given distinct boundaries of space and time. Most pretend play takes place in the designated areas of the classroom or on the playground outside. As a parent, however, I observed that the boundaries between real and pretend are not as distinct at home as they are at school. My own child didn't give me the courtesy of announcing when she was beginning and ending each play session. One minute she was my daughter and the next, suddenly and without warning, she could be a puppy or a dragon or even a snowball rolling down a snowy hill and gathering speed as she knocked me over on the living room rug. I suspect most children experience pretending at home a bit differently from pretending at school or in child care classrooms. At home, there is a freedom and spontaneity to play that is delightful to both children and their parents. Sometimes parenting a child who loves to pretend can be puzzling and frustrating but only because pretending is such a complex and fascinating process.

An invitation to play, such as "Let's pretend we're puppies," may seem plain and simple, even babyish, but pretend play actually involves challenging and abstract thought processes. When we pretend, one thing becomes a symbol for something else. When a child plays in a sandbox, a leaf is a plate, a stick is a spoon, a rock is a cookie, and the sand is the sugar that you sprinkle on top of the cookie before you bake it in the oven (which is a sun-warmed slab of stone next to the sandbox). When a child hands you the rock and says, "Here's your cookie, but be careful, it's still pretty hot," the child is engaging in an extremely sophisticated form of complex, abstract, and symbolic thought.

When we pretend, one thing becomes a symbol for something else.

In the field of education, teachers and other professionals often measure students' complexity of thought and level of cognitive challenge using a taxonomy developed by Benjamin Bloom (Anderson and Krathwohl 2001).

CREATING

EVALUATING

ANALYZING

APPLYING

UNDERSTANDING

REMEMBERING

(Anderson and Krathwohl 2001)

According to Bloom, the simplest and least complex thinking involves recall, memory, and rote learning. This is the lowest level of thinking on Bloom's taxonomy, "remembering." The teacher points to a circle and asks the student, "What shape is this?" and the student responds, "A circle." At the next level on Bloom's taxonomy is "understanding." The teacher asks the child to describe a circle and the child answers, "It's round." The child not only remembers the word "circle" but also understands at least one of the characteristics of a circle. As we progress up the levels of Bloom's taxonomy, the child's thinking becomes more and more complex, and the experience becomes richer and holds greater potential for advanced learning. Although Bloom did not consider play when he created his taxonomy, it's interesting to note that when children are engaged in even the simplest pretend play, they are already at least halfway up Bloom's taxonomy, because they are applying what they know about one thing to another thing, applying what they know about cookies and sugar to rocks and sand. In fact, you could argue that essentially all pretend play takes place at the highest level of Bloom's taxonomy, "creating," because pretend play, with its symbolism and inventiveness, involves creating something entirely new out of pretty much thin air.

Cognitive Growth through Pretend Play

Renowned educator and MacArthur Fellow Vivian Gussin Paley, in her book *A Child's Work: The Importance of Fantasy Play*, affirms the idea that pretend play, or what she calls "fantasy play," benefits children because of its sophistication and complexity: "The more complex the thought, the greater is the child's need to view its meaning through play and find the characters and situations that bring ideas to life" (2004, 57). Paley was referring to the child's need to dramatize or represent the ideas in her head through fantasy play. Paley also argues that the benefits of pretend play for children go beyond cognitive growth; pretend play offers social and emotional benefits that include intangibles such as comfort, friendship, and hope.

Children don't choose to pretend because it is a sophisticated pastime that will boost their IQ. They pretend because it's fun and it feels good.

They are driven to pretend because the experience is deeply satisfying emotionally and socially. Pretend play is as natural to children's growth as eating and sleeping. By taking on roles, children practice being in the world. Like a litter of wolf pups that stalk and wrestle with each other as they learn to become hunters, human children use pretend play to try out new language, actions, and ideas. Problem solving is an important part of almost every pretend-play scenario. How will the mommy help the hungry baby if the porridge is too hot to eat? How will the baby dolphins escape from the underwater jail made out of whale teeth? How will the superheroes rescue the president if the bad guys have surrounded the White House with hot lava? Much of the benefit of problem solving to children in these scenarios comes from the very real interactions they have with their playmates as they brainstorm and negotiate. One child will shout, "Help! Help! A monster is chasing us!" All is bedlam as the children scream and run, until another child shouts, "Here's a secret cave! Come hide in here!" The group takes shelter behind a tree. But before everyone has caught his breath, another child may shout, "Oh no, the monster can smell us and he's coming this way!" And they're off, encountering new challenges and creating new solutions at a rapid pace.

Pretend play is as natural to children's growth as eating and sleeping.

Pretend play also offers safe opportunities to try out ideas and feelings that might be too frightening to deal with in real life. Take our pirates, Jack and Rowan, in our opening scenario. They seemed to take great pleasure in making the teddy bear walk the plank, sending him to a watery, bloody death. The dark emotions and violence occasionally demonstrated in pretend play sometimes cause concern among adults, but, as I often assured parents when I was a preschool teacher, this is all normal human behavior. Better to express anger, jealousy, and frustration in the safe context of pretend play than to repress these feelings until they burst out in inappropriate ways. Teachers have an easier time with this pattern than parents do because we are able to observe from a professional distance.

I remember struggling with this issue as a parent. My daughter had a puppet made of terry cloth that she played with in the bathtub. One day, as I was helping her wash up, I put the puppet on my hand and made it say,

"Time to wash up!" My sweet little daughter took a bar of soap and shoved it in the puppet's mouth, squealing with laughter and saying, "Be quiet, stupid puppet!" I was surprised but played along. The puppet replied, "Hey! That's yucky soap!" This only inspired my daughter to further mayhem. For weeks afterward, every time she took a bath, she begged for the opportunity to torture that poor puppet with soapy violence. I vividly remember how much I did not enjoy that game. It was hard to watch my own child be cruel, even to an imaginary creature. I played along for a time because I understood it was normal and she needed the chance to play like that, but eventually I accidentally "lost" that puppet somewhere under the sink.

Imaginary Friendships

Another normal and appropriate way children process uncomfortable feelings is through the invention of an imaginary friend. In popular culture, one of the most familiar representations of a child's imaginary friend is in the comic strip *Calvin and Hobbes* by Bill Watterson. Calvin is the child and Hobbes is the imaginary friend. While Hobbes is based on an actual toy tiger, in the adventures Calvin and Hobbes share together Hobbes is much more active and animated than a small toy could ever be, demonstrating a more vivid and, at times, antagonistic role than a small toy could ever play. The relationship between Calvin and Hobbes, as Watterson has presented it, shares many similarities with the kinds of tumultuous relationships children often share with their imaginary friends. Hobbes frequently gives Calvin poor advice about how to behave or eggs him on when Calvin is considering mischief of one kind or another. Hobbes becomes a convenient, if not credible, scapegoat when Calvin is confronted by his angry and frustrated parents.

Many, but not all, children create imaginary friends, usually between the ages of three and six, the prime years for all kinds of pretend play. Often the imaginary friend, like Calvin's Hobbes, is naughty, clumsy, and immature. For example, in the classic publication *The Magic Years*, developmental psychologist Selma Fraiberg describes "Laughing Tiger," her young niece's imaginary friend. Laughing Tiger, unlike real tigers, did not roar. He was clumsy and bashful and he frequently forgot his manners and had to be reminded about how to behave properly. (One wonders if perhaps Bill Watterson had Laughing Tiger in mind when he created Calvin and Hobbes.) Fraiberg writes, "Now there is one place where you can meet a ferocious beast on your own terms and leave victorious. That place is the imagination" (Fraiberg 2008, 17).

Any concerns parents or professionals might have that the creation of an imaginary friend is somehow a sign of a deficiency in development is laid to rest by Marjorie Taylor in her 1999 book, *Imaginary Companions and the Children Who Create Them*: "The bottom line is that although imaginary companions and other fantasies have sometimes been interpreted as signs of emotional disturbance, a break with reality, or even the emergence of multiple personalities, they really are just a variation on the theme of all pretend play that is going on in the preschool years" (7). The imaginary friend in your child's life should be given the same warm welcome any young friend would receive in your household.

Observing children's play offers parents a window into their children's inner life—their hopes, fears, and interests. This is especially true when parents observe a child's interactions with an imaginary friend. Writer Adam Gopnik learned this when he listened in on his daughter's conversations with her imaginary friend, Charlie Ravioli. In a 2002 piece in the *New Yorker* titled "Bumping into Mr. Ravioli," Gopnik describes the relationship between his three-year-old daughter, Olivia, and Charlie Ravioli. "Olivia is growing up in Manhattan, and so Charlie Ravioli has a lot of local traits: he lives in an apartment 'on Madison and Lexington,' he dines on grilled chicken, fruit, and water. . . . But the most peculiarly local thing about Olivia's imaginary playmate is this: he is always too busy to play with

> *Observing children's play offers parents a window into their children's inner life—their hopes, fears, and interests.*

her. She holds her toy cell phone up to her ear, and we hear her talk into it: 'Ravioli? It's Olivia . . . It's Olivia. Come and play? O.K. Call me. Bye.' Then she snaps it shut, and shakes her head. 'I always get his machine,' she says" (Gopnik 2002, 80). Like Laughing Tiger, the imaginary friend of Fraiberg's niece a generation earlier, Charlie Ravioli is a reflection of the struggles and values of the time and place in which the child is growing up. Let's not wring our hands over the child who expresses her frustrations with and disappointments in the shortcomings of her imaginary companion; instead, let's rejoice that children have found such inventive ways to respond to the stresses in their environment.

Though children may raise their voices and knit their brows while they are engaged in pretend play, don't be fooled into thinking that pretending is a stressful experience. Pretending is sometimes a response to stress, but pretending is still play, a very satisfying and often very amusing type of play. If you have any memories of pretend play from your own childhood, you know this is true. One of my earliest memories of play is pretending to be lost kittens and puppies with my kindergarten friends. We took exquisite pleasure in trying to be the most dejected and traumatized animals. We were orphaned, frail, and had broken legs and broken tails. We were starving, ill with fevers and flus, and often blind. Frequently we died. I can still recall the immense joy of springing back to life again and starting the game anew.

Pretend Play Demonstrates Growth

Though we may refer to pretending as a game, there are few rules in pretend play. As Vivian Gussin Paley writes in *A Child's Work*, "From the earliest 'pretend I'm the mama and you're the baby,' play is the model for the life-long practice of trying out new ideas. Pretending is the most open-ended of all activities, providing the opportunity to escape the limitations of established rituals. *Pretending* enables us to ask 'What if?' " (Paley 2004, 92). The open-ended, creative nature of pretend play makes it one of the most sophisticated play experiences of childhood, an opportunity to create complex symbols and actions that represent very abstract concepts and stories. The idea that pretend play is a demonstration of abstract, symbolic thought challenges the conception that pretending is regressive, an infantile behavior. Pretending represents advancement. Over the course of early childhood, most children demonstrate advancements in their cognitive development through the progression of their pretend play, from the most concrete to the abstract.

Until infants and toddlers have developed language skills, they are not yet ready to participate in pretend play. They are working hard to understand the world in the most literal and concrete terms. When Daddy, as he moves the spoon to baby's mouth, says, "Here comes the airplane, *buzz buzz buzz!*," the baby may open his mouth because he loves the buzzing sound Daddy makes, not because he understands the spoon is a symbol for an airplane. Fraiberg asserts that language, as a symbol, is necessary for pretending and that most children do not develop the capacity for symbolic thought until they are about two years old (2008). When an eighteen-month-old plays peek-a-boo, for example, he really believes that, when his eyes are closed, others cannot see him.

As a parent, one of the first signs you will see that your child is developing the capacity to pretend is her effort to imitate you. And these days, usually one of the first actions children imitate is using a cell phone or a smartphone. Even as an infant, your child will hold a bar of soap or a cookie or toy up to her ear and imitate the actions she sees when her parents talk on the phone. When infants and toddlers imitate their parents like this, they are not pretending. They don't yet understand what a phone is and how it works. They are simply mimicking what they see. Your infant is not yet aware that when she holds her cookie up to her ear, she has a different experience than you have when you hold your phone up to your ear. The cookie is not a symbol representing a phone. Later, around the age of two and a half or three, children begin to understand simple symbols. A cookie can be a phone. The real pretending begins.

Children's first pretend adventures, at ages two and three, are usually based directly on the world around them. They pretend to be mommies and daddies and babies, brothers and sisters, aunties, uncles, and grandparents. The first pretend scenarios they act out involve the daily tasks they see performed around them, such as cooking and baking, giving the baby a bath, driving a car or riding a bus, buying food at the grocery store. As children gain more practice with pretending and their ability to communicate and use language gets a bit more advanced, usually in the middle of their third year, these "housekeeping" scenarios during pretend play will become more complex. More conflict and drama will occur. The babies will refuse to go to sleep, the daddies will come home late for dinner, the grandmas will burn the cookies, or the family will run out of food entirely. The best and most exciting pretend scenarios usually involve someone being naughty and getting punished.

As children continue to grow and develop, their pretend play will continue to get more complex and abstract. Instead of people, they will become animals, often the domestic pets they see in real life, or the animals they see in storybooks or on television and in movies. Many brave children will include monsters and other strange creatures in their play scenarios, or they may even become monsters themselves. Often the themes of danger and escape become important in preschoolers' pretend play, and these themes will continue through kindergarten and even primary grades, especially during outdoor play, when children enjoy running around and chasing each other.

Pretend Play in a Mass Media Culture

Superheroes and other characters from television, movies, and video games figure prominently in pretend play throughout childhood, and especially during the play of four- and five-year-olds. Sometimes children play the characters and the stories in ways that directly mirror what they have seen on the screen. But often they develop their own scenarios and dialogue. As an educator, I've often heard parents express concern that pretend play based on mass media franchises, such as Legos, Disney princesses, or Teenage Mutant Ninja Turtles, has no value and could, in fact, be harmful. Some parents worry that this kind of play is only rote imitation and that it reflects children's willingness to mindlessly follow the whims of a commercial and sometimes violent media culture. My response is to calm parents and ask them to try to observe their children's play objectively, paying close attention to the complexity, detail, and creativity that most children will bring to this kind of creative play. Earlier in the chapter I referred to Bloom's taxonomy and the many layers of complexity that children experience during play. When children take a mass media character, such as Batman, and develop their own pretend scenario, they are taking what they have learned from passively watching the show and actively applying it to a new, three-dimensional experience. By becoming actors in pretend play they are enjoying a fully kinesthetic and sensory experience, with greater meaning and complexity than anything they could experience during screen time. In most cases, the children are adding their own ideas, dialogue, and plot points; in doing so, they are creating an entirely new story, one that places them at the very pinnacle of complex thought, according to Bloom.

By becoming actors in pretend play they are enjoying a fully kinesthetic and sensory experience.

Another marker of sophistication in pretend play is the incorporation of magic. Unlike early examples of pretend play, such as cooking and driving, as children are mirroring what they see in their daily lives, when a child becomes a wizard with a wand that will change the broccoli into candy corn, the child is imagining a possibility that doesn't exist in real life. Magic in children's pretend play adds a new level of fantasy and creativity.

The Golden Age of Pretend Play

Five-year-olds are among the most creative pretenders. At this point in their development they have probably had several years' experience with pretend play under their belts. With any luck, they have been exposed to a broad range of source materials, from stories and fairy tales to TV shows and movies. Most have developed language skills that allow them to communicate well with their peers. Given time to develop their pretend scenarios, many children at this age will create stories with complex plot structures, often centered on a quest or a search for some kind of treasure or some form of rescue. During pretend play, children may begin to demonstrate their recognition that there are some gray areas between good and evil. A robber can help save a puppy. A fairy princess can be unkind and selfish. Children who have the pleasure of playing together frequently—friends at school, neighborhood friends, or siblings—may develop pretend play scenarios that build upon what has gone before, like chapters in a novel.

Protecting Pretend Play

After age five, as children enter elementary school and move through the often standardized instruction of the primary grades, pretend play begins to wane. Vivian Gussin Paley, in *A Child's Work: The Importance of Fantasy Play*, calls for educators (and parents) to protect and encourage pretend play. "We who value play must do more than complain of unwanted drills that steal away our time. We must find time for play . . . if we are to convince anyone of its importance" (Paley 2004, 33). One promising development in this area is the trend in education toward problem-based or scenario-based learning, in which students take on roles to research, brainstorm, and solve problems. This type of teacher-initiated learning can be imaginative and playful, though it is not the same as the child-initiated pretend play that is so characteristic of preschoolers and kindergartners. But if we broaden our definitions and understanding of pretend play to include problem-based learning and other kinds of role-playing, we can see that this type of play never really stops. Even as adults, we participate in pretending and fantasy, either actively or vicariously, through the books we read, the movies we watch, and the recreational games we play. An example is fantasy sports. Participants in fantasy sports leagues, such as football and baseball, create imaginary teams made up of real players. The success of the fantasy teams is based on statistics of the performance of the real players in real games. Millions of adults in the United States and Canada participate in fantasy sports.

And, of course, those of us who are parents get a chance to experience pretend play through our children. As a parent, watching my child pretending, and at times participating in pretend play with her, was one of the greatest pleasures of raising a young child.

The Parent's Role in Pretend Play

As Vivian Gussin Paley has described, the opportunities for pretend play at school are diminishing for many young children. The home is the final frontier of pretend play. Parents are in a powerful position to support, encourage, and participate in pretend play that excites and challenges children and supports their healthy development. Parents play a significant role in affirming and supporting their children's play by simply understanding the importance of pretend play and respecting it as a valuable pursuit. In their book *The House of Make-Believe: Children's Play and the Developing Imagination*, Dorothy Singer and Jerome Singer write, "Children experience psychological safety when they are accepted unconditionally and treated with empathy. They experience psychological freedom when caregivers allow them to express themselves symbolically and with few constraints. Children must not be teased or laughed at if their play appears silly or unrealistic" (Singer and Singer 1990, 153). As parents, we find it hard not to laugh with delight when our children are unintentionally adorable, but these authors are suggesting we should not intentionally make fun of our children and we should make an effort to demonstrate that we value children's pretend play.

Parents can demonstrate their respect and support for pretend play by managing some of the logistics regarding time, space, and props. Allow time for pretend scenarios to develop. For example, the pirate ship sailed by Jack and Rowan in our opening scenario took about twenty minutes to build, and the most dramatic and exciting moments in their play session didn't occur until a good thirty to forty minutes into play. If Jack's father had interrupted their play to serve breakfast or get them dressed, the story may never have come to fruition. Noticing when children are really absorbed in play and allowing time for their play sessions to develop is one way in which parents can support and respect their children's pretend play.

Providing space and props is another way parents can show their support for pretend play. The best play experiences often involve minimal or simple props. In the case of the pirate ship, the materials to build the ship included couch cushions and a flat sheet. Jack's sword was made from cardboard. There was nothing involved in the pirate play that had been purchased at a store for the purpose of playing pirates. Children often do enjoy colorful toys that are manufactured for a specific purpose. For example, dolls and stuffed animals are often at the center of children's pretend play. But when children incorporate household items into their pretend play—items such as bedding, brooms, old spoons or mixing bowls, broken umbrellas, or obsolete cell phones—they are not only challenged to engage their imaginations at deeper levels of abstract and symbolic thought, but they also get to experience the thrill, much like discovering a secret, of taking something unwanted or unnoticed by others and turning it into something that, in their own eyes, becomes really useful and valuable.

Gender Issues in Pretend Play

What about little boys who want to play dress-up? Questions about pretend play expressed by parents of young children are often related to gender and sexuality. Most parents want their children to be strong and capable, so parents of both boys and girls may grow concerned when they see their children take on roles during play that might be perceived as weak or passive. Unlike their parents, young children are not aware of the social, cultural, and sexual connotations. In most cases, the children are just curious. Parents should try to resist the urge to intervene. It's normal for young children to enjoy experimenting with different roles, characters, and props during pretend play.

What about girls or boys who want to prance about in their underwear, wiggling their bottoms like pop divas? Parents may feel uncomfortable when their children dance, move, or talk in ways that seem sexually suggestive. Usually the children are just imitating what they might have seen on television or in a movie and are not aware of how their actions are perceived by adults. But when parents react to children's pretend play with obvious discomfort, children sometimes react by taking an even greater interest in the play. If your child enjoys imitating a celebrity or character that you feel does not represent your family's values, be patient. Allow the play to continue, and be observant. At the same time, make sure that your child is exposed to stories and role models outside of mainstream pop culture. In my experience as a parent and an educator, the most valuable action we can take to support our children's play and learning and direct them to positive roles is to read to them from a wide variety of books. Fairy tales, folktales, and picture books provide the rich source material for pretend play and allow for some diversity and variation not often demonstrated on television and in movies. As Dorothy Singer and Jerome Singer suggest, "Of all the 'props' of childhood, none are more compelling or conducive to make-believe and fantasy than the books children read or hear read to them by a warm, loving adult" (Singer and Singer 1990, 15). Classic tales of good and evil, with captivating and charismatic animal characters such as bears, pigs, wolves, birds, and tigers, have a universal appeal that seems to inspire children across ages and cultures. Who wouldn't want to end the day as a furry or feathered creature, safe and snug with your fine animal family?

Running Around Like Crazy

The sky is gray with clouds and the path through the park is a sloppy, muddy mess. But Max, age four, and his sister, Piper, age five, laugh as they wade through the murky brown puddles in their tall rubber boots.

"Don't stomp or you might splash me," warns their mother.

"You should get boots like ours, Mommy," suggests Piper. "Then you wouldn't have to worry." Her mother sighs. She knows Piper's right; in her canvas shoes and light jacket, she's not dressed for a cool spring afternoon at the park. But as the trio approach the playground equipment, a bit of sun breaks through the clouds. Piper and Max take off running to the slide and their mother finds a dry spot on a bench, her face turned toward the sun.

"Chase me!" shouts Max as he climbs the ladder to the slide. Piper follows, calling, "I'm going to catch you up quick!" Max slides down the metal slope and, as soon as his feet touch the ground, he runs in a sprint to the ladder again. His rubber boots slow him down a bit on the ladder, but he makes it to the top, just out of reach as Piper climbs behind him. Up and down, they climb and slide, again and again, laughing and shouting, until it's not really clear who is chasing whom. When Max finally begins to tire of climbing the ladder, he wanders away from the slide and finds a long stick on the ground. He pokes the stick in a puddle and Piper soon joins him with her own long stick.

"Your stick is crooked," says Max. "Much crookeder than mine."

"No, it's not," says Piper. "That's just the reflection." She lifts her stick from the puddle and then pokes it back down, demonstrating how the reflection on the surface of the water distorts the shape of the stick, making it appear bent. "See?"

Max copies Piper's actions, moving his stick up and down. He accelerates the motion of his stick, up and down, until he is splashing the water with his stick.

"Max, be careful!" calls his mother from the bench. Max responds by running away, waving his stick in the air. He runs onto the grassy, soggy meadow next to the playground, where a small flock of geese have gathered, pecking at the soil with their beaks. Piper and her mother stand at the edge of the meadow watching Max chase the geese, waving his stick, until the geese take flight, honking, into the air. Max stands, watching the geese fly away, then runs to his mother and sister.

"Did you see that?!" he shouts. His mother notices the mud stains covering his knees and the front of his jacket, but instead of scolding she smiles, recognizing the joy on her son's face.

"I'll get you now, you little goose!" she calls to him as she starts chasing Max across the meadow.

"Me too!" calls Piper. "I'm a goose, too!" Their mother runs as well as she can in her thin canvas shoes, chasing both Piper and Max, no longer worrying about the mud and muck, just happy to be outdoors, enjoying the day with her children.

A big open space under a free wide sky invites us to run around like crazy. Children hear that invitation, loud and clear. They have a natural drive to move. Running, jumping, climbing, and spinning are essential play experiences because children just need to move their little bodies. They need it to grow, to stay healthy, to sleep well, to make friends, to have fun, to laugh, and to learn. When children move freely in active play, they hardly even know they are doing it. A small child like Max doesn't stop to think, "I'm going to run across this field and chase those geese with my stick." He's just following the will of his body and spirit, seeking the satisfying thrill of moving through an open space with freedom and joy.

While it's possible (and sometimes necessary) to run around like crazy indoors, with a roof over our heads, the outdoors is the best place for physical exercise and active play. The outdoors offers fresh air, wind, weather, trees and plants, animals, and people—sights and sounds and sensory experiences that can't be found indoors. A playground in a park, such as the one Max and Piper visited with their mother, offers all these lovely outdoor experiences, including mud and puddles, as well as the playground equipment.

In the lives of children, a playground is one of the most beloved locations. Equipment and structures such as swings, slides, teeter-totters, and monkey bars offer opportunities to move that can't be found in any other setting.

In the lives of children, a playground is one of the most beloved locations.

The sensation of swinging on a full-size swing set, for example, is both soothing and exciting, a deeply satisfying experience. Many playgrounds also offer features such as ladders to tall platforms, or sandboxes for digging, that provide views and textures and sensations that children are rarely able to experience at home.

For families with children from age two through seven or eight, the local park or playground can become the center of your universe, especially if you don't have a yard or outdoor space at home. I remember how, when my daughter was little, every time we drove by a park with playground equipment, no matter what neighborhood, no matter how far from home, she would ask, "Can we go there sometime?" As a working mom, one of the pleasures of the weekend was being able to spend a long time with my child at a park. She and I would often discuss and plan during the week, mulling over which parks we would like to visit during the upcoming weekend. Several times we planned what we called an "all park day," which meant we would spend the whole day going from one park to another. Each time we attempted to actually experience an all-park day, something kept us from being outdoors all day—rain in the forecast, an invitation to a birthday party, or just getting tired. At the time, I was disappointed that we never got to live our dream of the all-park day, but when I look back on it now, I realize that what we most enjoyed was the idea of it, the concept, the sense of possibility and freedom we experienced when we planned our all-park days. In reality, a good couple of hours was enough, and we were quite happy to come home, exhausted, our shoes full of sand from the sandbox.

My daughter was an only child, and parks and playgrounds were also important because those settings provided her with opportunities to play and interact with other children. Running around like crazy is so much more fun when you have other children to do it with. For many young children, friendships begin when they share a physical action—one runs and the other chases, one climbs and the other follows, one throws a ball and the other catches it. Children often engage in social play without any words at all, using only actions and movements.

The way young children engage with nature when they are outdoors is also very physical and active. Adults may enjoy sitting and watching birds flocking together in a field, but a young child like Max in our opening scenario, wants to run up to them. He doesn't intend to frighten or hurt the birds; he just wants to interact with them, to make something happen. Children want to touch and feel the world around them, especially when they are outdoors in the natural world of trees and plants and insects and animals. This is why children like to collect rocks and hold sticks and pick flowers. They want a piece of the world and they want to hold it and keep it. Playing with sand or dirt or leaves, digging holes, and making piles are some of the other tactile, sensory pleasures of being outdoors and experiencing nature.

The Benefits of Active Play

During the first five years of life, children's physical growth and development progress at a rapid pace. Infants usually become mobile at about six months, when they begin crawling, and soon are pulling themselves up into standing positions. Usually around their first birthdays, babies start walking. Most toddlers are driven to move and explore their world, punctuated by occasional breaks when they totter back to their parents and caregivers for reassurance and comfort. For young children learning to walk and navigate the world, this back-and-forth dance between independent exploration and the reassuring comfort of parents and caregivers can take place indoors or out, but there are even more intense pleasures and surprises to explore outdoors: a greater variety of smells, more variations in walking surfaces, more flowers and trees and plants and birds and dogs and worms to discover.

Between the ages of two and five, children's dexterity, coordination, and strength continue to develop quickly. Around age three, children are able to ride a tricycle, climb a ladder, and throw a ball. Around age four, most children are able to hop, jump, and climb. At age five, children can usually run well with balance and coordination, pump a swing, and hang upside down on the monkey bars. This amazing progress in physical development usually occurs fairly naturally when children have regular opportunities for active play. Exercise helps build strong hearts, muscles, and bones and can play a role in preventing disease. In recent years, the focus of many health organizations, such as Michelle Obama's "Let's Move!" initiative, has been on reversing the trend toward increased childhood obesity rates. Pediatricians and child health experts agree that every child should run around like crazy, each and every day.

Trends: Less Active Play Among Children

Most young children love to play and run around. So why so much concern about children's health and fitness related to exercise and physical activity, as demonstrated by the "Let's Move!" initiative? Much of the concern is directed toward school-age children above the age of five, whose play is not as spontaneous, free, and active as that of little children. But there is growing evidence that children of all ages are less active now than their parents' generation was at the same age. Research indicates that children today spend considerably less time outdoors than their parents did as children and that today's children are less likely to engage in spontaneous, child-initiated games and activities such as jumping rope or playing kickball (Clements 2004). Some of the possible reasons for this decline include the influence of television and digital media, concerns about crime and safety, and the increase in adult-structured activities such as organized sports and music lessons (Elkind 2007).

One possible remedy for the decline in physical activity is to reconnect children and families with the concept of active play. In an article titled

"Resurrecting Free Play in Young Children: Looking Beyond Fitness and Fatness to Attention, Affiliation, and Affect," physicians Hillary L. Burdette and Robert C. Whitaker propose that we stop telling children they need to exercise and start asking them what they want to play (Burdette and Whitaker 2005). "We propose that efforts to increase physical activity in young children might be more successful if physical activity is promoted using different language—encouraging play—and if a different set of outcomes are emphasized—aspects of child well-being other than physical health." A similar perspective is proposed by researcher Rhonda Clements in "An Investigation of the Status of Outdoor Play" (2004): "The most successful outdoor play experiences usually involve the child's free choice, which is self-motivated, enjoyable, and process-oriented. Natural experiences such as collecting leaves, throwing stones in a pond, jumping over small brush or logs, building sandcastles, collecting sticks or nuts from the ground, or creating hiding spaces challenge the child's imagination and reasoning abilities" (77). The message to parents is clear: if you want your children to be healthy and well, take them outside and let them play.

Two Model Solutions: Adventure Playgrounds and Outdoor Learning

For ideas and inspiration about how to engage children in the joy of outdoor, active play, parents and families can look to two successful models developed by professionals in the fields of education and recreation, one in the United Kingdom and one in the United States. In the United Kingdom, an organized network of "Adventure Playgrounds" provides opportunities for children to play outdoors in remarkably challenging and child-directed ways. What first caught my attention about adventure playgrounds is that children are allowed to build fires. That fact alone clearly distinguishes an adventure playground from the ordinary playgrounds I know in the United States. An adventure playground has no readymade equipment such as swings or slides. The children create whatever it is they need from the materials that are available, such as pieces of lumber, hay bales, large tubes or pipes, sand, and bricks. The idea of letting children play outdoors with discarded building materials and garbage makes a bit more sense when you learn that the British adventure playground concept grew out of efforts to create play spaces for children after World War II in areas of London that had been bombed during the war. These "junk playgrounds" were intentionally created for children on the sites of destroyed churches and schools (Kozlovsky 2008). Today there are many adventure playgrounds throughout the United Kingdom, operated through both public and private organizations. Such playgrounds are much more than open lots full of old bricks. Most adventure playgrounds are divided into several different kinds of play spaces, such as wild nature and planted areas, spaces for water and sand play, building and construction areas, and spaces for making fires and cooking outdoors.

While one of the primary concepts of adventure play is that the children should lead their own play experiences, it's important to note that every adventure playground is staffed by skilled "playworkers." The role of these adults is to facilitate play, not direct it. Play England, a British nonprofit providing resources and advocacy related to adventure playgrounds, defines the essential elements of an adventure playground as follows:

1 Spontaneous Free Expression: Children's spontaneity and drive to play means that the playground is in essence a space in which children have the freedom to determine the nature of their play.

2 Engagement in the Full Range of Play Types as Chosen by Children: The playground provides possibilities to engage in any and all play types.

3 Free Flow in Giving and Responding to Play Cues: Play is seen as an outcome in itself and children can engage in the full play cycle on their own terms.

4 Creating a Shared Flexible Space That Children Feel Has a Sense of Magic: The child's-eye view of what is special has precedence and the playground is co-created with the children. It is a fundamental aspect of the adventure playground ethos that children's "play in progress" is respected, for example by leaving camps and dens or other self-made creations in place so that their play can be resumed from where it left off.

5 Risk and Challenge: Children should be encouraged and supported to encounter and manage risk for themselves in an environment that is as safe as it needs to be rather than completely devoid of risk. The benefit to children of challenging play opportunities should be balanced with any potential risk when carrying out risk assessments.

(Play England 2009, 2,5)

Here in the United States, only a handful of British-style adventure play-grounds exist because liability concerns make it nearly impossible to open and operate them (Wiederholt 2006). But the concepts present in an adventure playground can inspire us to seek out similar experiences for our children in any outdoor space. We can allow children to take the lead and make their own choices during play, within reason, and encourage them, with safe supervision, to use found objects and repurposed construction materials to build and play. To me, one of the most intriguing aspects of the British model of adventure play is the care the play workers take to observe the children's verbal and nonverbal cues. "Play cues are the signals that children give through a spoken, facial, or other body signal or by the use of materials to indicate that they want to play. Engaging in the full play cycle means recognition that children's play may evolve and increase in complexity over time, and equally that play behaviours or props will be discarded when of no further use to their play" (Play England 2009, 2). So, for example, if a child picks up a shovel and begins digging, then sees another child with a hammer and wants to join her, that child's decision can be supported and her play facilitated by helping her find a second hammer. When children's spontaneous play choices are validated rather than discouraged, their play can develop into a more complex or more collaborative experience.

> We can allow children to take the lead and make their own choices during play.

In the United States, a quiet trend in education toward outdoor learning seems to be picking up steam. US and international initiatives focusing on children and nature include the Nature Action Collaborative for Children and the National Wildlife Foundation's "Get Outside" program (Wilson 2012). Educators and environmentalists, such as author Richard Louv (2012), argue that the cause of many difficulties with learning that students experience in traditional schools can be attributed to a lack of contact with nature and the outdoors. Classes taught outdoors are springing up at all grade levels, following in the footsteps of programs like Cedarsong Nature School, located near Seattle, the first "forest kindergarten" in the United States in which the entire school day takes place outdoors. Research supports outdoor education—students involved in nature-based learning programs have longer attention spans, better attendance, and higher academic achievement than their peers in traditional learning environments (Smith 2014). I believe the benefits of outdoor experiences for children are related to what Richard Louv describes as the multisensory experience of the outdoors (Louv 2012). The rich and varied sounds, smells, and textures children experience during outdoor play are in sharp contrast to the static indoor classroom that demands extended focus on the teacher or on an electronic screen. Not every family and community has access to forests and outdoor space, but the takeaway for parents in this discussion of outdoor learning is that children benefit from time outdoors on all levels of development—physical, social, and emotional, as well as cognitive and academic. If your child is struggling with academic learning, this could be a sign that she actually needs to spend less time with books and more time outdoors in a natural environment.

I remember when I was little, my father would say to my brothers and me, "You kids should go outside and run around." He said this often, but I don't remember ever actually going outside in response to his suggestion. Oh, we played outside all the time, but never because he suggested it. These entreaties usually came when he was tired or frustrated and probably needed a break from the noise of three children under one roof. What I do remember fondly are the times he went outside with us, especially to a park or playground. I loved it when he pushed me on the swing and played catch with me. Another vivid memory is the day he taught me to ride my bike without training wheels. He guided me down the street, pushing on the back of the bike, helping me get balanced. I'll never forget the moment I turned my head to say something and realized he had let go. I was riding the bike on my own and hadn't even realized it. What a terrifying and exhilarating moment! These memories confirm the significance of the time parents spend with children playing outdoors.

Chasing, Hunting, Seeking, Hiding

Parents, your children want you to play with them, not just watch them play. I know you're tired, but outdoor play is good for you, too. So stand up and move. You don't have to do much. Sure, your child wants you to run after her ("Chase me! Chase me!"), but you don't have to sprint all the way across the playground. Just make a good show of running and grabbing, making a few monster noises, and you'll do fine.

Young children enjoy any kind of chasing or searching game, such as the classic Hide-and-Seek. There are countless variations on this game, including Sardines (in which "it" hides first and all the players look for her and then each player who finds "it" joins her until all are hidden together) and Ghost in the Graveyard (essentially Hide-and-Seek played at night). Treasure hunts and scavenger hunts using hidden objects instead of hidden people also are fun outdoor games. The "treasures" needn't be valuable—a rock or even a paper cup from your picnic lunch could be hidden in the yard or park. You or your child could make up clues, draw a map, or just use the old "temperature" system, saying "colder" when the seeker moves farther away from the treasure, "warmer" as the seeker gets closer, and "hot!" when the treasure is close at hand.

For young children, pretend play and running around outside are an excellent pairing. Chasing games can be transformed by our imaginations from a simple game of Tag to an epic confrontation between good and evil, heroes and dragons. The wood chips at the bottom of the slide can become hot lava that will burn our feet if we don't run fast enough to the next piece of equipment.

The fascinating pleasures of the natural world, from beetles to birds, from sticks to sand, may require no enhancement for adults, but children are still inclined to build a fantasy scenario when playing outdoors. Soil and water become mud pies to feed the baby unicorns living in the bushes behind the sandbox. Ordinary sticks and leaves can be made into fairy houses with porches, doorways, and chimneys.

The Nature Connection

Very young children, ages two to five, usually do not need much convincing to go outside and play. Any resistance parents and caregivers might encounter often has more to do with the tricky logistics of navigating jackets and strollers. Once outside, young children are usually easily delighted by the outdoor world. As children get older, however, and the pull of electronic media and other distractions begins to cast a spell, children may need more encouragement to spend time outdoors. When this is the case, lectures about the benefits of physical exercise will fall on deaf ears. Focusing children's attention on nature, rather than exercise, can help cure their apathy about getting outside. For a child who does not like to run, especially an older child, give her a magnifying glass or a camera and invite her to look

Focusing children's attention on nature, rather than exercise, can help cure their apathy about getting outside.

for interesting and curious details in the environment. She will not run, but she will walk and explore and perhaps cover quite a bit more ground than she might have with only your cajoling to spur her on. Props and tools like the magnifying glass and camera can be used in any outdoor environment, including an urban setting where the influence of nature may be less obvious. Other tools might include binoculars, a sketchbook, or a bucket or bag for collecting things. For a child who does not like to draw, making crayon rubbings of various textures, on trees or on pavement, is an alternative to sketching or photography. As children get older, they will be less inclined to run around spontaneously and will benefit from being encouraged to simply walk and observe.

It may sound counterintuitive to suggest using technology to connect with nature, but there is a wealth of information and ideas for parents online. Many parents share ideas through blogs and social networking sites, such as Play Outside! (http://theplayfiles.blogspot.com.au). The social networking site Pinterest is another great source of images and ideas for outdoor activities, nature crafts, and things to collect.

The Risk Factor

When parents reminisce about outdoor play during their own childhood, one of the big differences we observe between when we were young and now is the design of playgrounds. The surfaces of American playgrounds now are almost always fully padded with wood chips or rubber mats or other kinds of cushioning materials. Gone are the teeter-totters that allowed your friend to jump off, leaving you to crash to the ground, bruising your tailbone on the hard wooden seat. Playground equipment, in general, is not as tall as it used to be, a reflection of concern over falls and injuries for children and the possible liability to the person or agency responsible for maintaining the playground. But in our efforts to make playgrounds safer for children, we have diluted some of the fun. For children, much of the pleasure of playing outdoors, running around like crazy, and climbing on playground equipment comes from the physical challenges they encounter and the satisfaction that comes from confronting fears and taking risks.

Psychology professor Ellen Sandseter asserts that children benefit from risky play because they progressively learn how to accurately judge risk and overcome challenges. She has identified six categories of risky play: "exploring heights, experiencing high speed, handling dangerous tools, being near dangerous elements (like water or fire), rough-and-tumble play (like wrestling), and wandering alone away from adult supervision" (Tierney 2011). Many educators and parents agree that most children need more experience testing their limits, taking risks, and dealing with failure. Science educator Ainissa Ramirez writes, "Children are innately risk-takers. If there is a curb, they will try to balance on it. If there is a shiny object, they will reach out for it. This is how they discover the world. Failure and risk-taking are how they learn. . . . We need to bring risk-taking back" (Ramirez 2013). Allowing children to take risks is a primary interest of parents who endorse "free-range" parenting. The term "free range" was coined by blogger mom Lenore Skenazy, who made headlines when she let her nine-year-old son ride the New York City subway alone (Larson 2012). She later penned the book *Free-Range Kids: How to Raise Safe, Self-Reliant Children (Without Going Nuts with Worry)*, describing her conviction that children should be allowed to take reasonable risks because it helps them develop independence and resilience (Skenazy 2010). This belief in the benefits of risk-taking is similar to the philosophy behind the British adventure playgrounds in which children build fires and use hammers, saws, and nails to create their own structures. This description of the essential element of risk in adventure playgrounds also makes for good advice to parents: "Children should be encouraged and supported to encounter and manage risk for themselves in an environment that is as safe as it needs to be rather than completely devoid of risk. The benefit to children of challenging play opportunities should be balanced with any potential risk when carrying out risk assessments" (Play England 2009). How each parent manages that balance between risk and safety will vary from family to family, but the main idea is that children must be active decision makers during outdoor play. We mustn't be afraid to let them take some initiative and make some of their own choices.

Here's an example of a small but important way that allowing children to make their own choices helps them to learn their own limits. In my first preschool teaching job, the school swing set had seats on hooks that could be raised or lowered along the chains that held the seats. The children were allowed to adjust the seats higher or lower, even though they sometimes pinched their fingers a bit during the process. Often children would become ambitious and raise the seat as high as they could reach, but then they were not able to do so. Many times they would ask a teacher to lift them up so they could climb into the seat. The school rule, however, was that the children could raise the seats as high as they wanted, as long as they could climb into the seats by themselves. The teachers could not lift them up. This rule was an effective "check and balance" measure that made sure the children did not climb higher than they could manage safely. The only time a child ever fell from a swing was when a parent who did not know the rule lifted a child into a high swing. Adults are often surprised by how much we can trust children to understand their own limits and abilities.

When my daughter was very little and still learning to talk, she liked to spin around in circles and then fall down on the ground. She'd laugh and say, "I'm so busy!" When she was a bit older, I tried to teach her that the word is actually "dizzy," but for a long time she refused to believe me, insisting that she was "very, very busy" each time she spun in circles until she couldn't stand up. I think she was right to stick to her guns. Spinning and rolling and running around like crazy, all kinds of active play, are important occupations for children, top priorities. So let's get busy!

CUDDLING SOMETHING SOFT AND SMALL

"Time for bed, Mister Furryhead," four-year-old Eli tells his small, brown teddy bear. Eli has just finished his bath and his mother has asked him to put on his pajamas while she gets Eli's baby brother ready for bed. Eli and Mister Furryhead are now left to their own devices in Eli's room. Instead of putting on his pajamas, Eli, still naked from his bath, makes an elaborate ritual of helping Mister Furryhead get ready to go to sleep.

"First you have to wash up," announces Eli. He lays the bear on top of the bed covers and pretends to pour water and soap on Mister Furryhead.

"Don't cry, Mister Furryhead," he says. "It's just a little soap."

Eli's mother walks by the doorway, holding Eli's little brother, who is fussing a bit. "Eli, what are you doing?" she asks. "Get your pajamas on."

"Mister Furryhead got some soap in his eyes, Mama," answers Eli. "He's crying too much. I have to help him." But Eli's mother is already down the hall, in the baby's room.

Eli picks up his teddy bear and holds it on his shoulder, just as Eli's mother was holding Eli's baby brother a moment ago. "There, there, Mister Furryhead," coos Eli. "It's okay. The crying washes out the soap in your eyes. Everybody knows that." Eli walks around the room, gently bouncing the bear. "Now you have really clean eyes, Mister Furryhead."

Next, Eli pretends to dress his bear in pajamas. In real life, Mister Furryhead wears no clothes, only his fine brown fur, but in Eli's imagination he's dressing him in a pair of red-and-blue Spider-Man pajamas.

"Eli!" calls his mother from the doorway. "Aren't you dressed yet?"

"Almost," answers Eli. "Mister Furryhead gets a little scared when his head gets stuck in the neck hole."

"In the what?" asks his mother. The baby has started crying again, so she leaves Eli's doorway and walks down the hall again.

"Time to tuck you in," Eli tells his bear. He places Mister Furryhead under the covers, the bear's head resting on the corner of the pillow. "I'll give you a lullaby in a minute but," Eli's voice takes a sterner tone, "you might have to wait for a while." Eli walks around the room in a circle, looking for his pajamas, and finds them on his chair, where his mother left them. Slowly, Eli puts on his pajamas, blue and red, with a Spider-Man logo. Eli is careful to center the neck hole over his head before he pulls on the pajama top, to make sure his head doesn't get stuck.

"I'll be right there pretty soon," Eli tells his teddy bear. "Don't you cry again, Mister Furryhead." Then Eli crawls into bed, his head next to his toy. "I can't be two places at once, you know," Eli whispers.

Eli cuddles up next to his teddy bear and begins singing, "Twinkle, twinkle, little star . . ." He sings the lullaby two times and is about to start on a third when his mother comes in the room, flips off the light, and kneels next to Eli's bed.

"That's a nice lullaby, Eli," says his mother, kissing his forehead.

"Shhh, Mister Furryhead is sleeping," replies Eli.

"Okay," whispers his mother. "Do you still want me to sing a lullaby to you?"

Eli nods and whispers, "But you have to be really, really quiet."

Eli's mother begins to sing in a soft whisper, "Twinkle, twinkle . . ." Before she finishes the song, Eli is asleep, still holding his furry bear.

A Universal Need to Cuddle

Cuddling a small, soft toy is an almost universal childhood experience. Most young children, from infancy through the preschool years, will, at some point, find a toy or soft object to hold that gives them comfort. Like Christopher Robin's Winnie the Pooh, the classic comfort toy, and like Eli's Mister Furryhead, the comforting toy is often a teddy bear, but any soft toy small enough for a very young child to hold and carry is an eligible candidate. A child may gravitate toward just one toy over a long period of time, and that toy becomes a special favorite. For example, when I was a child, my favorite cuddle toy was a fabric hand puppet I named "Sally." She had green braids for hair and yellow furry skin. Sally remained my favorite cuddle toy for many years. I would put her on my hand when I got into bed at night, and in the morning I was always a little bit disappointed to discover that Sally was no longer on my hand. She'd slip off sometime during the night, no matter how often I reminded her not to wander away. I recall sleeping with Sally well into my grade school years. Some children, like my daughter, for example, are serial cuddlers, switching from one favorite toy to another in fairly rapid succession. When she was a toddler, she seemed to prefer a terry cloth doll we called "Stripey Man." Later, she seemed to prefer Pinky Doll, then a blue teddy bear named Blueberry, and later still, Joey, a soft monkey with magnets in his hands and feet.

For some children, the preferred object of their affection is not a toy at all. Many children grow very fond of their baby blankets or other pieces of soft fabric. I knew a little boy who affectionately named his blanket "Cold," because the satin trim on the edges of the blanket felt cool to the touch. Sometimes the cuddle item is another household object, like a washcloth or even an oven mitt. Often a cuddle item is something that belongs to a parent, such as a scarf or a T-shirt. I recall a child who enjoyed carrying around one of his mother's nightgowns. She was a little embarrassed when he took this item to preschool with him, but when she saw how much he benefited from having it with him at naptime, she agreed to let him keep it.

In many parenting books, there is much attention, debate, and hand-wringing over what to do about such play items. Parents often have concerns over their children's dependence on their cuddle toys and wonder if they should be weaning their children away from this reliance. I'll address some of those concerns later in the chapter, but I'll say now that, frankly, I think the parenting literature misses a really important point about the meaning of children's relationships with their teddy bears, dolls, blankets, and so on. Simply put, children's interactions with their cuddle toys are play. They are playing at comforting another being, practicing being kind, helpful, tender, and compassionate. And what could be better than that?

This play experience, cuddling something soft and small, is very satisfying to young children because it is a comforting tactile and sensory experience. The visual appearance of the toy or object is not as significant as

> *They are playing at comforting another being, practicing being*
> *kind, helpful, tender, and compassionate.*

the texture and the smell (and sometimes the taste, as many very young children also suck on their cuddle toys). As discussed in Chapter 2, unlike an imaginary friend, who is often mischievous or naughty, in most cases the teddy bear, stuffed animal, or doll that is the object of the child's tender affections can do no wrong. This special friend requires and deserves as much care and attention as the child herself.

Cuddle Toys in Children's Literature

There are two great examples of stories about cuddle toys in contemporary children's literature. One is *Owen*, by Kevin Henkes, and *Knuffle Bunny*, by Mo Willems. In *Owen*, the title character is a little boy who is very fond of his yellow blanket. The text begins, "Owen had a fuzzy yellow blanket. He'd had it since he was a baby. He loved it with all his heart. 'Fuzzy goes where I go,' said Owen. And Fuzzy did. Upstairs, downstairs, in-between. Inside, outside, upside down" (Henkes 1993, 1–2). As the story continues, Mrs. Tweezers, the nosy neighbor, convinces Owen's parents to try various strategies to separate Owen from his blanket; for example, by soaking a corner in vinegar. Nothing works. When Owen grows old enough to go to school, his mother has the idea of cutting the blanket into handkerchief-sized pieces that he can carry in his pocket. In this storybook, Owen doesn't seem to mind when his mother slices his blanket with her sewing shears. After all, it is a work of fiction.

Mo Willem's *Knuffle Bunny*, another award-winning picture book, tells the story of a little girl named Trixie and her cuddle toy, a small stuffed animal named "Knuffle Bunny." Unlike Henkes's picture book, which takes place over a period of several years as it follows Owen's growth and maturation, *Knuffle Bunny* takes place on a single afternoon, during the time when Trixie is quite small. Her beloved bunny is accidentally loaded into a washing machine at the local Laundromat. Trixie is inconsolable until her parents are able to relocate her bunny in the wash, and the story ends happily. This short drama is very familiar to many parents of young children. The realism of *Knuffle Bunny* is less evident in Mo Willem's two sequels to this picture book, *Knuffle Bunny Too* and the final installment, *Knuffle Bunny Free*, in which Trixie gives her beloved bunny away to another child. Why do many authors end their stories about beloved toys and blankets by having the child somehow let go of it or of her attachment to it? Perhaps it's because so many parents are uncomfortable with their children's dependence on cuddle toys.

The Role of Cuddle Toys in Child Development

Parenting literature and child development texts usually include a great deal of information about the role of cuddle toys in the lives of young children. This is serious business, people. In the 1950s, a psychoanalyst named Donald Winnicott started something big when he established the term "transitional objects" in a 1953 paper, "Transitional Objects and Transitional Phenomena: A Study of the First Not-Me Possession." Here Winnicott described the value of children holding a beloved blankie, teddy, or doll for comfort and support as they grew and developed independence. The transition in the "transitional object" is the journey from dependence to independence, the gradual separation that infants make from parents as they begin to walk and navigate the world. Winnicott validated children's need to have and to hold a special blanket, cloth, or toy. As stated by Alicia Lieberman, renowned infant mental health expert, the transitional object is "a bridge between the mother and the external world" (Klass 2013).

In the half-century and more since Winnicott established the validity of the variety of children's playmates, from Blinky to Blanky, from Mr. Buns to Bunny Foo Foo, prominent pediatricians such as T. Berry Brazelton and William Sears have been working hard to convince parents that their children's attachment to that special toy or object is normal and healthy. In his classic parenting guide, *Touchpoints*, Brazelton states that children should be encouraged to develop a strong bond to a "lovey" such as a soft toy or blanket: "A child needs a comforting reminder from home and from the family relationship" (Brazelton and Sparrow 2001, 77). The parents of Henkes's picture book character, Owen, must not have read Brazelton's advice: "Parents may believe that because a child is in school now, she needs to give up a blanket, or a pacifier, or a thumb. This is not the time for such a step. This is a time to accept the need for regression as the child struggles to grow independent" (Brazelton and Sparrow 2001, 80).

Prominent pediatrician William Sears agrees. He advises parents not to try diversionary tactics that would manipulate the child into giving up a special object, such as replacing the lovey with a new, more age-appropriate item. Sears writes, "I don't recommend the trick of 'trading in' the blanket at a toy store in exchange for a toy." He states that comfort objects such as security blankets "cause no emotional or physical harm. Besides, you don't want to teach your child that attachments are easily disposable" (Sears 2014). As Sears suggests, the message most parents want to convey to their children is that relationships matter, especially tender, caring relationships.

Learning How to Love

When Eli, in our opening scenario, cradles Mister Furryhead and tucks him into bed, he is playing, but this is the kind of play that teaches children how to love and be loved. Sure, in psychoanalytic circles, cuddling a sweet, dear little thing may have clinical meaning related to the concepts of attachment and separation, but as parents, we only need our intuition to tell us that this is an experience that develops our children's capacity for kindness, empathy, and compassion. Pediatrician and author Perri Klass expresses this sentiment when she writes, "The familiar image of the small child and the transitional object, generally sweet and mildly humorous, occasionally frantic and even desperate, reminds us that learning to negotiate and even enjoy partings and reunions is part of the whole assignment, for parents and for children" (Klass 2013). This play experience is essential for all children, but probably especially for boys, who, as they grow up, will be allowed fewer and fewer opportunities by society to demonstrate kindness and caring. Societal expectations that boys don't cry, that they hide their emotions, that they are

All children, but particularly boys, need their families' support to experience play that represents the full range of human emotion.

tough and strong, will make it more difficult for them to express soft and tender feelings. All children, but particularly boys, need their families' support to experience play that represents the full range of human emotion.

Try This at Home: Supporting Cuddle Play

In the most practical terms, the best thing parents can do to support their children's play experiences involving cuddling soft toys and other comfort items is not to get in their way. Let them do it. In fact, the American Academy of Pediatrics (AAP) advises parents to take an active role in helping their child choose a transitional object: "Despite myths to the contrary, transitional objects are not a sign of weakness or insecurity, and there's no reason to keep your child from using one. In fact, a transitional object can be so helpful that you may want to help him choose one and build it into his nighttime ritual" (American Academy of Pediatrics 2014). The AAP also directs parents to gird themselves against the Knuffle Bunny–ish trauma of the missing toy by buying two identical objects. "Doing this will allow you to wash one while the other is being used, thus sparing your baby (and yourself) a potential emotional crisis and a very bedraggled lovey. If your baby chooses a large blanket for his security object, you can easily turn it into two by cutting it in half. He has little sense of size and won't notice the change. If he's chosen a toy instead, try to find a duplicate as soon as possible. If you don't start rotating them early, your child may refuse the second one because it feels too new and foreign."

I tend to join Perri Klass, however, in her skepticism that parents can control the mysterious whims of a child in search of a cuddle toy. As soon as you purchase two identical bears, the child will attach herself to an old pillowcase with a peculiar stain that can't be replicated. "Some parents are able to 'suggest' a convenient object (and buy multiples to keep in reserve), but children are guided mostly by their own mysterious and passionate preferences, and they do not necessarily accept substitutes—witness all those stories about turning the car around to go back for the one true blankie" (Klass

2013). The most special of special items has to be selected by the child and the child alone.

This doesn't mean the parent abdicates all power and authority to the child. Parents can still set clear and age-appropriate limits on how and when the special cuddle toy can be carried and played with. There will be moments, such as posing for the family's holiday portrait, when a child should not be allowed to hold a toy. As a child gets older, he can begin to share the responsibility for keeping track of the special toy. A four-year-old, for example, is probably old enough to keep track of the cuddle toy's location within your home, but will still need help making sure the toy is accounted for when venturing out into the wide world on outings or vacations.

One of the saddest family stories I've heard was from the parents of a five-year-old who discovered as their plane was taking off that their child's special toy had been left behind at the airport. The parents felt helpless because there was nothing they could do to retrieve the toy. I had the experience myself, as a child, of losing a special toy named "Sticky Icky," a soft plastic creature covered in suction cups, while on vacation. My brothers and I were playing in the garden of a vacation cottage, and I playfully buried Sticky Icky in the loose soil, like a game of Hide-and-Seek. When it was time to unbury the toy I somehow was not able to find it again. We had to leave the cottage to go home without my toy. I comforted myself by deciding that my Sticky Icky would grow, like a seed planted in the soil, into a beautiful flower. When a beloved toy is lost, children learn to deal with the loss. Such pain and sadness are part of learning compassion and caring.

Sometimes the loss of a special toy is even harder on the parents than on the child. Even when the child gradually grows less and less dependent upon or interested in the cuddle toy, due to healthy development and naturally increasing independence, parents may feel pangs of sadness and nostalgia when their child no longer holds or carries the special cuddle toy. I'm certain that the children's story *The Velveteen Rabbit*, in which a discarded old rabbit toy is transformed through magic into a real rabbit, was actually written for parents, to comfort us as we watch our children grow up. It is a bittersweet pleasure to see our children become more independent. It is what we wanted all along and feared would never happen, and yet sometimes we want to just hold them again, soft and vulnerable in our arms, the same way they held their cuddle toys.

All Cuddled Creatures, Great and Small

As children grow older, their desire to cuddle and care for something soft and small is sometimes directed toward real animals, such as the family or classroom pet. This is an excellent way for children to continue to develop their capacity for kindness, compassion, and empathy. Patty Born Selly has written extensively on this topic in her book *Connecting Animals and Children in Early Childhood*: "It's been my experience, and the research certainly bears it out, that animals can help children develop sensitivity to others, they can offer comfort, and they can even provide a safe sounding board for secrets and feelings that children don't share with adults" (Selly 2014, 2). Selly also suggests that children's interactions with real animals can help them overcome some of the traditional gender roles about caregiving behaviors mentioned earlier in this chapter. Selly asserts that the experience of caring for an animal can be especially valuable for boys: "Researchers have found support that boys are socially conditioned against being caregivers at a very young age. Animals provide boys with the opportunity to care for and nurture something" (Selly 2014, 156). While all children may enjoy and benefit from the experience of holding a puppy, feeding a hamster, or petting a kitten, these experiences may be of particular value to boys because, as they grow older, they will have fewer opportunities than girls to share these experiences through play.

Laughing, Joking, and Other General Silliness

Six-year-old Annika is helping her father with a project, sticking adhesive address labels onto plain envelopes. She works carefully, making sure to place each label correctly in the center of each envelope. When they finish labeling the large box of envelopes, Annika's father moves the empty box from the table to the floor, smiles at his daughter in appreciation, and says, "Well, I'm glad we're done with that box."

Annika smiles back at him and then her smile widens into a grin and a twinkle of mischief shines in her eyes. She leans over, lifts the box from the floor, and places it back on the table. Annika's father grins back. He lifts the lid of the box, feigns surprise at discovering the box is empty, and returns it to the floor, repeating, in exactly the same tone, "Well, I'm glad we're done with that box."

Annika smiles and lifts the box again and the silly drama repeats—the raised lid, the surprise, and again, the punch line to their new joke, "Well, I'm glad we're done with that box." Except this time Annika's father escalates the joke by placing the box in a new location—on top of the refrigerator, out of Annika's immediate reach. He sits back at the table and pretends to busy himself with the envelopes, watching Annika out of the corner of his eye. Annika fetches the step stool from the kitchen pantry, places it next to the refrigerator, and climbs up, safely retrieving the empty envelope box and placing it back on the table in front of her father.

Annika's father waits until Annika has returned the step stool to the pantry and has sat back down at the table before he pretends to notice the box, looks under the lid, and proclaims, deadpan, "Well, I'm glad we're done with that box." Annika laughs out loud, while her father tries hard not to crack up. This time, he lifts the box and carries it upstairs. Annika does not follow; she seems to appreciate the escalating rhythm and pattern of their joke. She will wait until he returns and then look for the box. Annika's father comes back to the table, without the box, *whistling an idle tune. He grins to himself when Annika takes off up the stairs. It takes her a good five minutes to find the box, which he had hidden in the bathtub, behind the shower curtain. She returns, triumphant, and places it back on the table. When her father pretends to be startled, jumping in his chair at the sight of the box, and proclaims, "Well, I'm glad we're done with that box!," they both burst out laughing. The spell has been broken, the jig is up, but they couldn't be happier.*

What's So Funny?

A baby's first smile and first laugh are joyous milestones. As a parent, the silly play and wacky fun, the laughter and the jokes, will be among the happiest moments you share with your child. In early childhood, our definition of "funny" includes everything that makes a child laugh, from slapstick physical actions to silly sounds, from word play to jokes, from comic strips to comedy films. Joking around, laughing, and being silly are essential play experiences because they are so enjoyable and are often very social activities that connect children with friends and family.

What a young child finds funny (such as farty noises) is often very different from what an adult finds funny (such as stand-up comedy on HBO). But as Annika and her father illustrate in our opening scenario, there is much common ground to be enjoyed in families and between parents and children. The playful game that develops between Annika and her father demonstrates a number of concepts that help us define humor and understand how it develops in young children. For example, all humor is contextual. What's funny in one place and time may not be funny in another place and time. In the classic Road Runner cartoons, we laugh when Wile E. Coyote gets hit on the head with an anvil, but we would not find it funny if that happened to a real person. We can laugh at a pratfall or slapstick physical comedy as long as no one is actually getting hurt.

The relevance of context in humor is universal; it is important to what both adults and children find funny. For example, the funny exchange that developed between Annika and her father took place after they had been working hard together, with serious focus, to complete the task of sticking labels on envelopes. If the game had developed at a different time in a different context, the humor and fun would have been tempered. For example, if Annika had been getting ready for bed and her father had been tired, he probably would have viewed Annika's playful manipulations of the envelope box as a frustrating diversion intended to delay bedtime. In the actual context, however, Annika had essentially earned this moment of silly play because it followed a period of serious work and concentration. For both Annika and her father, the funny exchange involving the box was a relief and release from their work.

Another universal element of humor is surprise. We laugh when we encounter something that is unexpected, incongruous, exaggerated, or novel. A joke is funny when we don't already know the punch line, or when the joke is delivered in an entirely novel way. For example, the first type of joke that many children learn to tell is the knock-knock joke. It follows a simple pattern that begins with the words "Knock, knock," announcing that someone or something is knocking on a door. The setup and structure of the joke (the required response, "Who's there?") create the expectation that we'll soon find out who or what is on the other side of the door. But often there is a twist or word play involved that transforms the exchange into something else, surprising us.

Here's a classic example:

"Knock, knock."

"Who's there?"

"Boo!"

"Boo who?"

"Why are you crying?"

We laugh when we encounter something that is unexpected, incongruous, exaggerated, or novel.

I worked with a kindergarten class in which the children became particularly enamored of the "interrupting cow" family of knock-knock jokes. The joke requires a more advanced level of skill because timing is an important element.

"Knock, knock."

"Who's there?"

"Interrupting cow."

"Interrupting c—"

"[Interrupting] Moo!"

The first time I heard the joke, the child delivered it very well and I thought it was hilarious. I was truly surprised. Over the next few weeks, many of the children in the class learned the joke and loved telling it to me over and over again. Although the surprise was lost, I enjoyed observing how the children practiced and learned to deliver the punch line quickly enough to successfully interrupt the speaker. They also enjoyed creating a series of variations on the cow joke. We had a whole barnyard of animals knocking on our door—interrupting pig, interrupting horse, interrupting rooster, interrupting dog, interrupting cat, even interrupting mouse. Although we all knew the structure of the joke and were not surprised by the interruption, there was still a sense of surprise in anticipating when the interruption would come.

Another universal element of humor, similar to a sense of surprise, is incongruity. Funny faces, silly dances, and slapstick actions such as dropping a tray of dishes, make us laugh not only because they are unexpected but also because they are a distortion or an exaggeration of the normal experience. From Charlie Chaplin to Carol Burnette to Robin Williams, many of the most beloved comedians in film and television have been those who were able to make us laugh by using slapstick, physical humor that surprises and delights us without any words at all.

Any of these incongruous, surprising experiences become funnier when we share the humor with other people. Young children enjoy silly, funny play most when they are interacting with other children or with their parents and other family members. A sense of humor is an essential social skill. Most of us, as adults, have fond childhood memories of laughing uncontrollably with siblings or friends, a funny moment that had us laughing so hard we were, literally or figuratively, peeing our pants or making milk come out our nose. Making funny faces and cracking jokes is a great way to make a new friend, to connect to the people you love, or to defuse a tense situation.

How Funny Grows: The Development of a Sense of Humor

As children grow from giggling infants to wisecracking teenagers, their cognitive development progresses to allow them to understand humor in increasingly complex and sophisticated ways. At the same time, their physical development, their language and social skills, and their emotional maturity progress in ways that allow them to actively use humor, tell jokes, and make others laugh. While there's some evidence that even newborn babies have the capacity to laugh (*Medical News Today* 2004), most parents begin to enjoy making their babies crack up when the babies reach about four or five months.

If you're ever curious about what makes babies laugh, just check out YouTube. The prevalence of laughing-baby videos on that site seems to have started around 2007, with a short, sweet video of a Swedish dad making funny noises while his son, who looks to be about six months old, sits in a high chair and laughs gleefully. Each time the laughter dies down, the dad makes another beepy, silly sound and the baby begins laughing all over again. The video became a viral Internet sensation and has logged more than fifty million views. Since that time, laughing-baby videos seem to be a particular online favorite, especially the videos of twin babies cracking each other up. Even if you're not a fan of YouTube, it's hard not to be enchanted by the sight of a little baby laughing. The only thing better is watching your very own little baby laughing. And the things that make babies laugh are pretty universal: surprises (bubbles, dogs, spinning toys), unusual sounds (sneezes, crinkling paper), and getting tickled or "booped" on the belly.

The experience of watching a bunch of videos of laughing babies in quick succession really emphasizes the fine line between laughing and screaming. One moment the baby looks terrified, eyes wide with fright, and the next she is smiling and shrieking with laughter. The babies often look at the faces of parents as if to say, "This one's funny, right?" Babies observe the body language and facial expressions of their parents and caregivers as cues for interpreting the meaning of the events happening around them, to determine whether they should be amused or afraid. Babies' natural sensitivity to the moods and responses of others also contributes to the infectious nature of laughter among infants and young children. Laughter can be contagious among babies and children—one starts laughing and the others laugh at the laughter. I recall my own experience observing this phenomenon when my daughter was a baby and we would visit the swings at the local playground. When the three or four baby swings were all filled with happy babies, my daughter would often become so enchanted by the laughter and happy screams of the other babies around her that she sometimes didn't even need me to push her swing at all. She was happy just to watch the other babies, laughing, clapping, her little legs kicking with delight at the fun she saw all around her.

As children become more active and mobile, from toddlers to walkers to runners, they continue to work on the important developmental task of determining the difference between fearful and funny. As parents, we can see them dance between terror and hilarity when they insist that we chase them. One moment the child is laughing, egging us on as we chase him, pretending to be a monster or a bear, and the next moment he dissolves into tears, overcome by the intensity of that moment.

Taking More Control of Their Humor

As children grow from toddlers to preschoolers, they become, literally, more active in their experiences with humor, and they begin to take more control and more initiative. The game of Peek-a-Boo, for example, can be a source of laughter and fun for babies and young children. Parents often initiate Peek-a-Boo with their babies, but in the toddler years, children begin to gain the upper hand. Toddlers who are two or three often enjoy jumping out from under covers or from behind trees to startle and surprise their parents and friends. Children are often particularly delighted when the adult feigns exaggerated surprise and shock. "Oh, there you are! I didn't see you there!"

At around the age of two, children also begin to understand and enjoy the humor of things that are incongruous or out of place. Take, for example, the toddler who cracks herself up by putting her cereal bowl on her head. Kids love it when their parents play along or create their own incongruous humor. If you don't believe me, put your gloves on your feet and your socks on your hands and see how many three-years-olds will laugh at you. Finding the funny in things that don't make sense is a silly but important milestone of childhood; it means that children have developed enough intellect to understand what the normal or standard uses of common household items are and can recognize when something is out of place.

Another incongruity children enjoy is related to physical humor, the way we distort our faces and bodies when we're being silly. At ages two and three, children are likely to take the initiative in the funny face and silly noise department, often surpassing their parents in this regard. Children enjoy sticking out their tongues, making "raspberry" sounds, and taking pratfalls, just for the silly fun of it. At this age, as they begin to learn language and develop the ability to have longer and more complex conversations with their parents, children are often able to say things that make their parents laugh, both intentionally and unintentionally. Just as on the vintage radio and television show *Kids Say the Darndest Things*, young children charm and amuse us with their misunderstandings, mispronunciations, uncensored honesty, and bewildering non sequiturs. Take, for example, this conversation between a mother and her three-year-old daughter, which took place while the little girl was sitting on the toilet:

Lily: Mommy, we are almost out of toilet paper.

Lily's Mom: Well, I'll get some more out of the closet.

Lily: Okay. Thank you. Hey! I was just thinking . . . I wonder what it would be like to sit on a fish.

Lily's mom couldn't help but laugh out loud at this odd suggestion. In this case, Lily recognized after she spoke that her musings about a fish were a little silly. Sometimes, however, when children are expressing their ideas in earnest and expect to be taken seriously, parents must try very hard not to laugh at their children's mistakes or misconceptions. Here's an example of a four-year-old boy having what he perceives as a serious conversation with his mother about dinosaurs.

Jake: Mom, people used to run away from dinosaurs all the time.

Jake's Mom: Well, buddy, did you know that dinosaurs and people were not on Earth at the same time?

Jake: What? Why not?

Jake's Mom: A long time ago, they all died.

Jake: WHY?!?

Jake's Mom: Different scientists have different hypotheses—like something really big fell from the sky, or they all got really sick, or the temperature changed a lot.

Jake: I have a hypothesis, Mommy.

Jake's Mom: Really? Great—tell me about it.

Jake: Poison frogs. They fell from the sky.

Jake's Mom: [pause] What?

Jake: Yep. That was it, Mommy. Poison frogs.

In this case, Jake's mother could tell from his tone of voice that Jake really wanted to have a serious conversation about an important matter. She had to work very hard not to laugh and to listen carefully to Jake's idea. This anecdote serves as a great reminder that often what children want most from their parents is their undivided attention, without distraction from other people or cell phones.

Around the age of three or four, when many children make their first attempts at telling an actual joke, with a punch line, one of the grand motivations to tell jokes is the focused attention children receive from others while they are telling the joke. A child with older siblings learns this quickly. Take, for example, three-year-old Lucy, who is riding in the car with her parents and older sisters. One sister tells a joke she heard at school: "What do you call a pig that knows karate? A pork chop!" Lucy laughs along with the rest of her family, even though she doesn't quite get the joke. Then Lucy announces, "I have a joke!" She is delighted to have everyone's attention and loves the way her older sisters turn toward her, faces bright, ready to listen. It doesn't matter that Lucy doesn't know any jokes yet, she just wants to be part of the fun. "What's your joke, Lucy-loo?" her father asks. Lucy responds with the funniest, silliest thing she can think to say, "Poo poo poopy head!" Her family laughs and a true comedian is born. It won't be long before Lucy comes up with additional and, eventually, more sophisticated jokes.

When children begin learning to tell jokes, the "knock-knock" structure is popular because it is very simple and replicable. Years ago, when I was a preschool teacher of a class of three-year-olds, I invited the children in my class to tell me jokes and many of the jokes they told began with "Knock, knock." Here are two examples of original knock-knock jokes from our class:

"Knock, knock."
"Who's there?"
"Froggie."
"Froggie who?"
"Silly froggie."

"Knock, knock."
"Who's there?"
"Boo koo."
"Boo koo who?"
"Boo koo koo who."

> *The "knock-knock" structure is popular because it is very simple and replicable.*

Another popular structure of the original jokes in our preschool joke book was the explanation joke, a question-and-answer format similar to the classic joke:

"Why did the chicken cross the road?"
"To get to the other side."

Here is a variation on that original joke as told by one of the preschoolers:

"Why does the Barbie roller-skate?"
"Because she loves to roller-skate."

This Barbie joke is a clear variation of the chicken joke and follows very similar logic and structure. I admit it's not especially funny. Like the chicken joke, the surprise is not that it's incongruous; the surprise is that it actually makes sense. The child who made up the Barbie joke expertly followed the model.

Here's another example from our preschool joke book:

"How did the elephant get in the refrigerator?"
"There were footprints in the butter."
"Why did the chicken cross the road?"
"Because of the footprints in the butter!"

I find this example hilarious and intriguing. In the first half of the joke, the child is trying to retell the classic joke that usually goes something like this:

"How do you know if an elephant has been in your refrigerator?"
"You find footprints in the butter."

Our preschool jokester can't quite get it right and distorts both the question and the response. But she doesn't stop there! She goes on to what seems like a whole new joke, the classic chicken joke. And instead of delivering the expected punch line, she goes back to the punch line from the first flubbed joke. This joke was very well received among both the preschool children and their parents. It was funny in its earnest and surprising mistakes and distortions and it brilliantly demonstrates the messy and hilarious process of learning to tell a joke.

"Real" Jokes and Sophisticated Word Play

When children get a bit older, as they enter grade school and start learning the conventions of reading and writing, some of the silly spontaneity of preschool humor is lost. What's gained, though, as children learn to accurately retell the jokes they've read or heard on TV or from their friends, is a growing sophistication in their understanding and appreciation of humor. From school age to adulthood, much of the humor in jokes and stories comes from an incongruity or unexpected element in the meaning, sound, or spelling of words. Examples of humor based on the incongruous or unexpected are puns. A pun is a form of word play or joke in which a word or phrase has more than one meaning, or sounds like a word or phrase with a different meaning. For example, in the sentence, "When a clock is hungry, it goes back four seconds," the pun is in the phrase "goes back four seconds." In the context of a clock, "seconds" means a measure of time. But the phrase also sounds like "goes back for seconds," the expression that means to get another helping of food. Children usually develop the ability to understand puns around the age of eight or nine. The incongruity caused by the multiple meanings in puns, as well as the word play in riddles and story jokes, is much more sophisticated than the simple novelty and surprise that amuse younger children. To appreciate puns and riddles, children must be

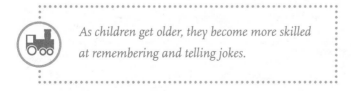

As children get older, they become more skilled at remembering and telling jokes.

old enough to have achieved what psychologist Jean Piaget called the "operational stage" in cognitive development. Research affirms that operational thinking is necessary to comprehend and appreciate humor that is based on a violation of cognitive expectancies (McGhee 1971). As children get older, their comprehension skills and vocabulary increase, and they become more skilled at understanding, remembering, and communicating jokes, including puns and riddles.

Most school-age children seem to enjoy hearing and making up riddles based on structured rules or patterns. For example, the PBS series *Zoom* taught many children how to enjoy and create a form of riddle called "Fannee Doolees." To get a Fannee Doolee riddle, you have to know how to spell.

> *"Fannee Doolee swims in a pool but not at the beach.*
> *Why do you think that is?"*
>
> *or*
>
> *"Fannee Doolee sleeps on a pillow but not in a bed. How could that be?"*

"The trick to FaNNEE DOOlEE is that she likes anything with double leT-Ters. So, she likes swEEts but doesn't like candy" (PBS Kids 2014). She likes bees and butterflies but doesn't like ants or spiders. Fannee Doolee likes riddles but doesn't like jokes. Making up your own Fannee Doolee is a great demonstration of word play and the ability to understand that a joke can be based on both the meaning of a word and the spelling of the same word.

Along with the maturation of their cognitive abilities, children in elementary school and middle school are more aware of the social contexts for humor. What a child considers to be funny is often greatly influenced by what other children think is funny. Preteenagers and teenagers enjoy

What a child considers to be funny is often greatly influenced by what other children think is funny.

having "inside" jokes with their friends and may be reluctant to joke around with their parents or other adults. Parents may feel left out and miss the fun they had with their children when they were younger. Older children and teenagers may even be embarrassed by their parents' attempts at jokes and humor, but families can still laugh together by watching funny TV shows or movies or by playing funny group or board games, such as Apples to Apples, Balderdash, or Taboo. (Games for families to enjoy together are discussed in great detail in chapter 7.)

The Funny Family

Just as each person develops his or her unique sense of humor, every family is different in how its members enjoy or express humor. A family's culture and beliefs can influence how and when family members make jokes, act silly, and laugh. In some families, humor would be out of place, even disrespectful, during certain events, meals, or rituals. In other families, humor is used to express affection and defuse tension even in the most important moments and events, such as weddings or funerals. Young children observe and absorb their families' practices and traditions, but, in general and across cultures, children tend toward funny business more frequently and with greater gusto than adults do. As parents, much of the pleasure of spending time with our children is in the laughter they inspire.

The following is a list of funny books recommended for parents and children to enjoy together, especially for the read-aloud crowd, ages two through six.

Some Suggested Funny Read-Aloud Books

Bad Kitty by Nick Bruel

Bark, George by Jules Feiffer

A Couple of Boys Have the Best Week Ever by Marla Frazee

Diary of a Worm by Doreen Cronin

Don't Let the Pigeon Drive the Bus! by Mo Willems

Duck! Rabbit! by Amy Krouse Rosenthal

Frankenstein Makes a Sandwich by Adam Rex

Good Night, Gorilla by Peggy Rathmann

Hi, Pizza Man! by Virginia Walter

Moo, Baa, La La La! by Sandra Boynton

Take Me Out of the Bathtub and Other Silly Dilly Songs by Alan Katz

This Is Not My Hat by Jon Klassen

Today I Will Fly! by Mo Willems

Some Funny Books for Independent Readers

Amelia Bedelia series by Peggy Parish

Captain Underpants series by Dav Pilkey

Junie B. Jones series by Barbara Park

A Series of Unfortunate Events series by Lemony Snicket

Stinky Cheese Man and Other Fairly Stupid Tales by Jon Scieszka

Some Jokes to Share

"Knock, knock."

"Who's there?"

"Tank."

"Tank who?"

"You're welcome!"

"Which side of a dog has the most hair?"

"The outside."

"Why do sharks live in salt water?"

"Because pepper makes them sneeze."

"How did the barber win the race?"

"He knew a shortcut."

"What did one eye say to the other?"

"Don't look now, but something between us smells."

"Why is 6 afraid of 7?"
"Because 7 8 9."

"What did zero say to 8?"
"Nice belt!"

"Why do bees have sticky hair?"
"Because they use honeycombs."

And a Few Puns

- I've been to the dentist many times, so I know the drill.
- I stayed up all night to watch the sun rise, and then it dawned on me.
- Being struck by lightning is a shocking experience!
- Past, present, and future got into an argument. It was tense.
- Two antennas met on a roof, fell in love, and got married. The ceremony wasn't much, but the reception was terrific.
- Cannibals like to meat people.
- The coffee tasted like mud. It was fresh ground.
- Two silk worms had a race. They ended in a tie.

Creating a Beautiful Mess

It's "poison time" in the Wilson family kitchen. Three-year-old Noah and his older brother, Brody, age five, assemble a collection of bowls, plastic containers, and mixing spoons on the kitchen table while their father stands at the counter chopping vegetables for dinner. Noah and Brody know the routine—their parents have set aside these stained or worn cooking items for the boys to use for messy play. They store them, clean and ready to use, in a bin under the table. Noah and Brody's parents let them create concoctions using whatever kitchen utensils and ingredients are no longer needed by their family. The boys usually begin each messy play session by mixing a bit of flour and water while their father or mother rummages through the refrigerator or cupboards for stale food items the boys can safely add, such as an expired bottle of ketchup. The boys like to call this play "making poison" because they know they shouldn't try to eat or even taste their concoctions.

Today, Noah and Brody are especially excited to make poison because their father has given them some stale seasonings to use in their recipes: a shaker of oregano and a small container of nutmeg. The play begins in the usual way when their father gives each of his sons about a cup of plain flour. Brody adds water from a small plastic pitcher and begins stirring with a spoon, making a paste, but Noah wants to touch the dry powder with his fingers first.

"Soft, soft poison," says Noah, poking and patting the flour with his fingers.

Brody adds a bit more water to his flour, turning it from a paste to a sauce. Then he opens the small container of nutmeg.

"Try smelling that nutmeg, Brody," suggests his father.

Brody takes a big sniff. "Uck!" he says, making a face. "That stuff has a tickly smell."

"Let me try," says Noah, reaching for the nutmeg.

"No!" says Brody. "You take this one." Brody hands Noah the shaker of oregano.

"I want to smell the 'meg," Noah persists. Brody holds the container of nutmeg to Noah's nose. "Mmm," says Noah. "Smells like cookies."

"Then you take this one." Brody gives Noah the nutmeg and keeps the oregano for himself. Noah seems satisfied with the exchange. The boys add their flavorings to their mixtures, sniffing and stirring. Brody looks into Noah's bowl. "You need water, Noah."

"No, I don't," says Noah. "I'm making it dry. For dry poison. To sprinkle on the most terriblest cookies."

"Me, too," says Brody. "I'm making terrible cookies, too."

Noah smiles, clearly pleased that his older brother wants to copy his idea. "Daddy?" asks Noah. "Can we bake our terrible cookies in the oven?"

"For real or pretend?" asks his father.

"For real, for hot," answers Noah. "Just to see."

"Not tonight, buddy," says his father. "I need the real oven to bake the pasta. But you can pretend. Where should your pretend oven be?"

"On the chair!" exclaims Brody. He and Noah place their containers of poison on a kitchen chair.

"Set the timer, Daddy," says Noah.

"How long do your cookies need to bake?" their father asks.

"Twenty-forty minutes," replies Noah.

"Got it," says the boys' father, setting the kitchen timer for two minutes.

Noah watches the timer while Brody watches the poison cookies bake in the oven. Brody smiles at his father. "These cookies will definitely be the worst we ever made, right, Daddy."

"Right," agrees their father, nodding his approval. "The worst ever."

The Intentional Mess

Young children are notorious for making messes. For parents of little ones, there's just no avoiding it. Much of the chaos of parenting young children comes from the unintentional messes children leave in their wake—they're just too young to keep their toys and socks organized, and their mouths and hands simply don't work well enough yet to stay clean during meals. But there's another kind of mess that comes from play—the beautiful, creative, and intentional messes children make when they are using all their senses to explore and learn, the messes made with play materials like clay, paints, mud, bubbles, and sand. These are the messes we talk about when we talk about essential play experiences.

In early childhood, often the best messes are the wet messes.

In early childhood, often the best messes are the wet messes. Outdoors, natural materials like dirt and sand can be transformed into exciting play experiences by just adding water. Children are often fascinated by the ways the consistency of a substance like mud changes depending upon how much water has been added to the mix. This is why the sandbox or garden makes a fantastic laboratory for messy play. Indoors, kitchens make great settings for play with food items or art materials, and bathrooms, especially those with bathtubs, are perfect for wet, soapy play with bubbles and foam.

Not all messes are wet. Like Noah in our opening scenario, some children are also inspired to play with dry substances, such as flour and sand. Creative play projects can incorporate many dry art materials, such as paper and yarn. A dry mess made with paper and scissors will require a broom instead of a mop for cleanup, but children still gain many of the same valuable benefits from a dry mess as they would from a wet mess.

Sometimes it's hard to tell the difference between productive messy play and just plain making mischief. Context is everything. Smearing paper with fingerpaints is okay, but smearing the bathroom wall with toothpaste is not okay. Stacking wiggly gelatin squares into towers at a birthday party is okay, but building a fort out of your meatloaf and mashed potatoes in a fancy restaurant is not okay. These distinctions can be confusing for both

Sometimes it's hard to tell the difference between productive messy play and just plain making mischief. Context is everything.

children and parents. Messy play that involves edible ingredients is particularly tricky because different families have different values, culturally and economically, about how food should and should not be used by children in play. In the Wilson family, for example, as described in our opening scenario, Noah and Brody's parents let the boys use fresh flour as a play material, but only let them add other ingredients that are stale or ready to be discarded. In some families, particularly when family members have experienced hunger or food insecurity, every bit of food is eaten and no food item is ever used for play.

When messy play is called "art" and incorporates materials purchased as "art supplies," there is some clarity of purpose and intent. Fingerpaints are supposed to be touched and poked and smooshed. Clay and playdough are supposed to be patted and pounded and rolled. Among the happiest memories of my own childhood is the memory of painting at an easel. I vividly recall the satisfying and sensory experience of plunging the thick paintbrush into a cup of paint and sweeping the soaked bristles across the page, with thick slow drips of paint rolling down the paper. Another happy memory of childhood is the smell of brand-new crayons and the pleasure of opening the box and seeing and touching the unsullied tips. The first drawing a child makes with a fresh box of crayons or a fresh box of markers always feels special.

Making messes, an essential play experience, includes any two-dimensional drawing or painting and any three-dimensional sculpture made of clay or wire or cardboard or toothpicks and glue. I use the word "mess" to describe the freedom of movement and playful experimentation involved in these projects and experiences; the finished piece or project may not turn out to be quite orderly and balanced. Many of these artful messes created by children are uniquely beautiful.

Sound in Messy Play

Much of the pleasure of messy play comes from the way it engages our senses, primarily seeing, touching, and smelling. But hearing, listening to sound, is another important sense involved in healthy, messy, productive play. Bev Bos, early childhood educator, author, and fan of messy play, in her book *Don't Move the Muffin Tins*, suggests that rubber dog toys make great painting implements for young children (1978). Dip a dog toy in paint and press it on paper. Not only do you get to feel the squish and see the pattern it makes on the page, you also get to hear the squeak! That's a great example of a multisensory experience. Sound alone can be a fun plaything. Making noise is another excellent form of messy play.

When children shout, sing, hum, whistle, or stomp, they are playing with their voices or using their own bodies as toys or playthings. Some toys, such as bells, keyboards, and drums, are manufactured for the purpose of playing with sound. Household objects can also become noisy playthings and musical instruments in the hands of young children. When my daughter was little, a cardboard shoebox became a favorite drum that she played off and on for years. Early childhood educators agree that experimenting with sound is a valuable educational experience for young children and helps them learn about their world. "When offered a variety of drums and strikers, children play with sound. By exploring and 'messing around,' they discover they can make one sound by striking one drum and a different sound by striking another" (Kemple, Batey, and Hartle 2004, 31).

Noisy play may be educational and entertaining for children, but loud noises can be frustrating and annoying for adults. Rosemary Wells's children's book *Noisy Nora* illustrates this point. Nora is the troublesome middle child in a family of mice. She creates a ruckus in the house to gain attention and, it seems, to playfully entertain herself with a variety of sounds:

First she banged the window,
Then she slammed the door,
Then she dropped her sister's marbles on the kitchen floor.
(Wells 1999)

Messes made with sounds are similar to messes made with sand or clay or paper, in that it is often hard for parents to tell the difference between productive play and mischief. As a general rule, play is either joyful, with delight visible on children's faces, or very focused, with a concentration and unself-consciousness that is very different from the watchful vigilance of a child who is intentionally acting out. Discerning the differences between a legitimate mess and a mischievous mess is an important parenting task, because there's much to be gained by allowing your children to make legitimate messes.

The Many Benefits of Messy Play

Early childhood educators and child development professionals have a fancy term for making messes; we call it "sensory play." Educators know that children learn best when many of their senses are engaged—not just sight and sound but certainly touch, and, if possible, smell and taste. That's the way babies learn about the world, by reaching and touching and putting things in their mouths. Messy play with loose, wet, and malleable materials, such as sand, clay, and paint, teaches children about the properties and characteristics of matter. The science of playdough (or really any liquids or solids used in open-ended play) includes the concepts of mass, volume, and dimension, although in early childhood we are more likely to discuss these concepts with children in terms such as more and less, full and empty, heavy and light. Developmental psychologist Jean Piaget observed children's play with messy and wet materials and formed some conclusions about the significant milestones of children's cognitive development in the early years. Piaget observed that between the ages of four and seven, most children develop the beginnings of "operational" or logical thought and that a turning point in this process is demonstrated in the child's ability to master "conservation," the ability to understand that redistributing material, such as pouring water from a flat, wide glass into a tall, thin glass, does not affect its mass or volume. While most four-year-old and many five-year-old children will think that there is more water in the tall glass, because it is "higher" than the other glass, most seven-year-olds understand the principles of conservation and know that when water is poured into a different-shaped glass, the quantity of liquid remains the same (McLeod 2010). The best way to master these concepts is by messing around with water and other liquids, loose materials such as sand, and soft solids such as mud or clay.

Messy play also helps children develop physical strength and coordination as they dig and squish and pound and carry. Small-motor skills, the kind that will help children develop a comfortable and balanced pencil grasp as they learn to write, are supported and developed when children draw with crayons and markers and when they hold paintbrushes. Messy play is often a very social activity, something shared with other children and family members, which gives children practice communicating, negotiating, and solving problems. In her article "Let Them Throw Cake: Messy Kids May Be Faster Learners," science writer Belinda Luscombe spotlights research that looked at how infants learned when they were allowed to get their hands dirty and make a mess with nonsolid objects such as oatmeal and applesauce. The researchers found that the babies who made the biggest messes, or, in other words, who used their hands the most to touch, taste, and smell the substances, were better able to learn the names for the substances than the babies who didn't make a mess (Luscombe 2013). Messy play may also be beneficial to children's emotional health. Like adults who squeeze soft stress balls to help them relax, children who engage in messy play with soft and malleable materials may experience emotional benefits. "As children squeeze and pound clay, they release tensions and relieve stress" (University of North Carolina at Greensboro 2014). Among preschool teachers, a common strategy for defusing conflict and discontent among children is to open up the water table, playdough center, or sandbox, and allow children to work through their frustrations safely, using the messy materials to push and pull, pour and stir. The experience can be very soothing.

We never really outgrow the pleasures of kneading and pouring. As adults, we might seek out activities like cooking, gardening, or even washing dishes because we enjoy the sensory aspects of such experiences. As children grow older, they gradually become more goal-directed in their messy play and art projects, moving from a focus on process to an interest in product. When they are very young, usually from infancy through around age four or five, they don't begin a project with a preconceived notion or vision for what they are creating. If you ask a three-year-old standing at an easel, dripping paintbrush in hand, "What are you painting?," she will probably ignore you. She is moving the paint from cup to paper for the pure pleasure of doing so. Gradually, as children's cognitive development advances and their experience and knowledge of the world increase, they may begin to make short-term plans as they play. "I'm making a river," a child may announce, as she digs a long channel in the beach sand. Eventually children will approach messy play with clear intent. They want to create a painting or clay sculpture that represents something they can imagine in their heads. They begin working toward that goal as they play.

One of the great gifts of messy play is that there's so much room for experimentation and mistakes. A clay sculpture that starts out as a dog can easily be turned into a cat, or flattened and squeezed into a snake. Clay and dough and other messy play materials are very forgiving. This is a low-risk, safe activity for children. There are no right or wrong answers. Learning to make mistakes and to recover from them is one of the most important life lessons, one with which many adults still struggle. Learning from their mistakes and even celebrating them is a valuable experience for young children at the beginning of their school years. The ceramic artist Beatrice Wood, who has worked with clay her whole life, is frequently quoted as saying, "My life is full of mistakes. They're like pebbles that make a good road." Whether using pebbles, clay, paint, or sand, we need these messy, sensory experiences to help us prepare for the road ahead.

The Reluctant Child

While most children will eagerly step in the mud puddle, splash in the tub, and stir the sticky bowl full of dough, some children may be hesitant to touch gooey messes. Perhaps their disposition or natural preference leans toward order and cleanliness, perhaps they are worried they'll get in trouble if they make a mess, or perhaps they just haven't had much experience with sensory activities. A little encouragement may be all that's needed before the child dives in and enjoys making messes. For some children, sensitivity to particular textures and sensations will make them extremely reluctant to play with sand or other messy substances. Do not force children to touch or play with messy materials. Be patient and give them time to observe you or other children making messes. Offer them items such as sticks, brushes, or utensils that they can use to manipulate the messy materials without touching them directly. Continue to offer the materials for play on a regular basis, and over time reluctant children may choose to engage more and more deeply in the process.

Tips and Ideas for Making Messes at Home

I know a mom who has a "No playdough" rule in her home. She does not want pieces of playdough to get stuck in her nice rugs, so she has banned the substance completely from her home. Her reasoning is that her two children, still preschoolers, can play with playdough almost every day at preschool, so they aren't missing out on anything. I respect this mom's decision. While I'm tempted to suggest to her that her children could still play with playdough on their patio or in the laundry room, I hold my tongue because I know that each of us, as parents, must draw the lines where we see fit. My rugs aren't nearly as nice as hers, so who am I to judge?

One of my favorite messy memories from childhood was when my mother allowed my brothers and me to "write" on the kitchen table with our frozen fudge pops. She would first wash the linoleum tabletop with soap and water, so it was pretty much as clean as any of our plates or bowls. Then my two brothers and I, dressed in old play clothes, would sit at the table and begin licking our fudge pops. Then we would start drawing or writing on the table, using the fudge pops like paintbrushes dripped in chocolate paint. We'd lick and draw and drip and use our fingers to spread the sticky ice cream all around until the entire tabletop was covered with chocolate. I don't remember what happened next, but I suspect we were probably sent outside to be rinsed off with the hose or into the bathroom to be wiped up with a big wet towel or actually put into the bath. Painting with the fudge pops was a special activity in our family and probably only happened a handful of times, but it was exciting for me and my brothers, and it demonstrated to me the importance of creating safe spaces for free, messy play in our homes.

For parents, the practical considerations for messy play will vary a bit depending on the ages and interests of your children, the amount of space you have available, and how easy it is to clean the surfaces in your play space. Make sure both you and your children have a set of play clothes that are okay for getting dirty or stained. For painting, a big shirt can be used as a smock, but messy play with wet ingredients can soak through a smock pretty quickly, so sometimes it's better just to wear old clothes. In some families, children are allowed to be naked during messy play with paints or water or dough. That certainly saves on laundry!

The kitchen floor is usually a good surface for messy play with very young children. For art projects, a table or easel provides a surface for paper and paints. If an easy-clean floor area is not available, a shower curtain or vinyl sheet can be spread on top of a carpeted floor to protect it. A large plastic wading pool can also be used indoors to create a space for messy play. You can even set up the painting easel inside the empty pool.

Plastic bins make great storage for paints, brushes, and messy play supplies. Set aside a bin for collecting wet or dirty brushes and toys so they can be carried to the sink to clean, without leaving drips behind. Involve children in the cleanup process. Preschool teachers know that rinsing the paintbrushes is one of the most popular cleanup jobs among young children. It's like a bonus play session. Children are fascinated by the mix of colors in the soapy water, and the process of rinsing can make cleaning soothing and satisfying.

Being "Green" in Messy Play

Many parents are vigilant about waste and seek to be efficient and economical in their use of food and resources. Rather than purchasing special supplies and materials for children's messy play, families can use items found in nature or reuse materials that are no longer needed for their original purpose. A home recycling bin can provide families with plastic containers for water, sand, or paints, as well as paper for covering floors or for making a doughy pulp for play.

Using materials from nature for play is the theme of Marjorie Winslow's delightful book, published back in 1961, *Mud Pies and Other Recipes: A Cookbook for Dolls.*

The whimsical recipes include dishes such as "Roast Rocks," "Dandelion Soufflé," "Bark Sandwich," and "Leaves en Brochette." The book is a curious mix of child-centered playfulness and adult-centered humor. For example, the recipe for "Mud Puddle Soup" is very childlike in its simplicity. All you do is find a mud puddle after a rainstorm. But the next recipe, "Mock Mud Puddle Soup," seems to parody the popular cookbooks of the time. To make this "mock" soup, you must dig a hole and run the hose into it. Winslow suggests, "This kind needs a little seasoning, so add a pinch of the dirt that you dug out" (7). Although the cookbook was written more than fifty years ago, the emphasis on using what you can find outdoors or around the house reflects a contemporary "green" sensibility. For example, Winslow suggests, "Cooking utensils should, whenever possible, be made from something that would otherwise be thrown away. . . . The bottom half of a heavy cardboard egg carton does nicely as a muffin tin and as a mold for individual cakes and pies." This is advice parents and children can still heed today.

Join the Mess!

Parents play an important role in the setting up and cleaning up of messy play, but they can also be important participants. Children's enjoyment and learning are enhanced when their parents engage with them in any play experience. During messy projects, like painting or playing with clay, adults can model different motions or techniques, such as rolling a piece of clay into a long, thin snake. They can engage in conversation by making observations ("I see how the yellow paint is mixing with the other colors") and by asking questions ("What do you think will happen when the yellow and the red mix together?"). Children often enjoy including their parents and play-mates in pretend scenarios during messy play, such as inviting their parents to "taste" their delicious mud pies and sand cookies.

Recipes for Messy Play

For children ages three to five, here are three great homemade options for indoor or outdoor messy play: playdough, fingerpaints, and the substance commonly known among the preschool crowd as "goop."

Playdough

This is the recipe I used as a preschool teacher. It makes a nice soft dough that, if stored in an airtight container, lasts for at least a week. When my daughter was little, we often made this together at home. She helped with the stirring and kneading, with careful supervision during the cooking on the stove.

Ingredients

2 cups flour
2 cups warm water
1 cup salt
2 tablespoons vegetable oil
1 tablespoon cream of tartar
Liquid food coloring

Directions

Mix all the ingredients except the food coloring in a skillet or pan and stir over low heat. The dough will begin to thicken until it resembles lumpy mashed potatoes. When the dough pulls away from the sides, remove from heat (or turn off the heat in the electric skillet) and let it sit until it's cool enough to handle. Then knead the dough, adding drops of food coloring until you reach the desired color and consistency.

Fingerpaints

Commercial fingerpaint can be expensive and smelly. Here's a homemade alternative. The recipe is very similar to the playdough recipe, but the desired consistency is much wetter and gooier.

Ingredients
2 cups flour
2 teaspoons salt
2 ½ cups cold water
2 cups boiling water
Liquid food coloring

Directions
Mix the flour and salt in a bowl. Add the cold water and stir until smooth. Prepare the boiling water in a saucepan and gradually add the mixture from the bowl to the boiling water. Boil until the mixture becomes smooth and thick. Use a whisk to eliminate lumps. Add drops of food coloring until you reach the desired color. Cool completely before allowing children to touch the fingerpaint.

"Goop"

Goop is a slimy, rubbery substance that goes by many names. Some call it "Silly Putty" and others call it "Gak" or "slime." It's fun to make and play with, but it can harden and stick to surfaces, so don't leave it on your antique side table overnight. Goop is fun to squeeze and twist. My preschoolers also enjoyed cutting it with scissors.

Ingredients
½ cup white glue (or one 4-ounce bottle)
1½ cups water, divided
Liquid food coloring
1 teaspoon 20 Mule Team Borax laundry detergent booster

Directions

In one bowl, mix the glue and ½ cup of water and add a few drops of food coloring. In another bowl, dissolve the Borax in 1 cup warm water. Gradually add the glue mixture to the Borax mixture, stirring slowly. Soon it will be too thick to stir, so use your hands to knead until the mixture is completely combined. Don't worry if there's extra liquid in the bottom of the bowl; just discard whatever is left. Store in an airtight container or zipper storage bag.

"No-Mess" Options for Messy Play

Sometimes, for very practical reasons, such as sharing your living space with other human beings who don't value messes as much as children do, messy play is just not an option. Even when paint, clay, mud, or sand is not available, children can still enjoy playing with water, especially in the bathtub. Adding "no tears" bubble bath or even a few drops of mild dish soap will add fun and intrigue to your child's bath experience. In addition to, or as an alternative to, store-bought bath toys, children enjoy playing in the tub with kitchen items such as colanders, spoons, ladles, whisks, and turkey basters. Children also really enjoy playing with foam shaving cream, holding it and squishing it in their fingers or spreading and patting it on the walls or sides of the tub.

Another no-mess alternative to playing with messy materials is to play with sound and music, especially outdoors, where there's less concern about disturbing other people. Toy instruments such as drums and bells are fun for very young children, even infants and toddlers. Preschoolers and older children can mess around with toy or child-size versions of keyboards, guitars, and harmonicas. Homemade musical instruments can be created out of boxes, bins, and cartons. A jar or tub filled with beans or rice can become a shaker. A coffee can or box can become a drum played with hands or with sticks. Young children enjoy just messing around with sounds, experimenting with cause and effect. Older children can be challenged to make up sound effects or mood music for a story from a book or from their own imagination.

Parents can encourage children by offering to record their sounds or music. Many smartphones have an audio recording option.

For inspiration, check out the innovative music video "Experiments around the House," by the musical duo Lullatone:

www.lullatone.com/news/experiments-around-the-house.

And finally, if you're looking for a perfectly clean and quiet way for your child to make a mess, you could always play with light. A flashlight or projector can make a mess of light on any surface, and children enjoy experimenting with shadows and reflections. Show your child how to make hand shadows or try using different toys and objects to create shadow stories on a wall or ceiling. Mirrors and other reflective surfaces can add complexity to light play.

> *If you're looking for a perfectly clean and quiet way for your child to make a mess, you could always play with light.*

The Joy of Messes

For many children, messy play is their very favorite kind of play. There is a crazy joy to it, a freedom to move and feel in new and exciting ways that is similar to the thrill of running around, jumping, and spinning. Imagine the excitement, then, when messy play and running around outside are combined into a single experience. The classic children's book *A Hole Is to Dig: A First Book of First Definitions*, written by Ruth Krauss (1952), and illustrated by Maurice Sendak, captures this thrill when the children explain, "Mud is to jump in and slide in and yell doodleedoodleedoo!"

Playing Turn-Taking Games

 *"I call camels! I want to be the camels!" exclaims Ellie as she opens the game box. Ellie, along with her older sister, Kate, is preparing to play Parcheesi with her mom and dad. Parcheesi is a classic board game that Ellie and Kate's parents played with their families when they were little. This contemporary version has pawn pieces shaped like animals—camels, tigers, elephants, and water buffalo.*

"I'll be the tigers," says eight-year-old Kate. The elephants are claimed by Kate and Ellie's mom, which leaves the water buffalo for their dad.

"Ellie, the camels start here," Kate directs her sister. Ellie has played this game before, but at the age of four she still needs a lot of assistance from her family to participate. The object of the game is to move each of your pawns all the way around the board to "home." Each move is determined by a roll of the dice. But there are a number of rules that make the play more complex and challenging than just following a path. For example, you must roll a five in order to start each pawn and begin moving along the path. Luck plays a significant role in the game; if you roll "doublets," a pair of matching dice, you get a bonus turn. The game also includes opportunities to capture or block other players.

Ellie hasn't mastered the game yet, but she still enjoys being part of the fun, so her family finds ways to assist her. For example, early in the game, Ellie gets frustrated because she hasn't yet rolled a five and her camels are still stuck at Start, so when Ellie's mom takes her turn and rolls double fives, she "gives" one of her fives to Ellie.

"That's not in the rules," protests Kate.

"Our family has our own Parcheesi rules," explains their dad.

Kate is willing to let it go. She enjoys helping Ellie count the spaces as she moves her pawns around the board. At one point in the game, Kate even points out to her sister a way she could block their mom's elephants.

"Ha!" says Ellie to her mom. "Camels are better than elephants, aren't they, Mama?"

"We'll see," says her mom, smiling.

In the end, Kate wins the game, gathering all her tigers at the Home space in the center of the board. With just a few minor tweaks for Ellie, they have played the game fair and square.

"Let's play again!" suggests Ellie.

Her mom checks the clock. "Goodness! We've been playing for a whole hour. Time for bed."

"Can we play Parcheesi again tomorrow?" asks Kate.

"We'll see," answers her mom.

"Maybe I could be the tigers next time, right, Kate?" asks Ellie. "Those camels are too slow."

"Dad," whispers Kate, so Ellie won't hear. "The animal you pick doesn't make you win or lose, right?"

Her dad pats her on the back. "Yep, you're right. Ellie will eventually figure that out, too. Just give her time."

"Okay, Dad," says Kate, smiling, enjoying her role as the older sister and sharing this secret with her dad.

Games for All Ages

"Fun for the whole family" is a common phrase used in advertising for vacations, amusement parks, and shows, and often these venues have very steep ticket prices. A family game night, however, costs very little and generates real, actual fun, as demonstrated by Ellie and Kate's family's experience playing Parcheesi. A board game is a great equalizer among family members of various ages, from small children to adults, offering many intergenerational pleasures, such as challenge, humor, and surprise. Board games are just one type of game children enjoy. Families with children of all ages play card games, dice games, word games, guessing games, party games, and

> *Most games have rules, a goal or object,*
> *and they are fun.*

car games. These are all games usually played indoors. Outdoors, children enjoy playground games, such as Tag or Mother May I?, or sports games, such as baseball, tennis, or soccer.

Games are a special category of play. The common characteristics of games are that they have rules, they have a goal or an object, they often have a winner, and they are almost always fun. Most games are played in groups or in pairs. Some games are played on computers or using electronic game devices, and games that incorporate technology will be discussed in chapter 10. Here we will focus on games that children and families are likely to play together.

Learning to Play Games

To participate in games, children must be old enough to communicate, follow rules, respond to challenges, and, in some cases, accept the outcome of the game, whether it is winning or losing. Most children do not begin developing the skills and maturity to participate in an organized or structured game until they are four or five years old. If you've ever tried to play a game of Duck, Duck, Goose with a group of three- or four-year-olds, you know exactly what I mean. To play Duck, Duck, Goose, the players sit in a circle on the floor or on the ground. The person who is "it" walks around the outside of the circle, tapping each person on the head. With each tap, she says "duck." At some point during the circling process, as "it" taps and says, "Duck, duck, duck, duck . . . ," one of the seated players will hear, instead of "duck," the word "goose!" That person must stand up quickly and chase "it" around the outside of the circle and try to tag her before she reaches the empty spot in the circle and sits down. If the runner (or "goose") can't catch her, the runner becomes "it." Very young children enjoy this game very much, but are not always able to follow the rules. When Duck, Duck, Goose is played with three- or four-year-olds, several things are likely to happen.

1 The person who is "it" will enjoy tapping and circling so much that she will never say "goose."

2 One of the seated players will be so excited and eager to run that she will stand up and start running, even if she has not been selected as the "goose."

3 The person who does get to be the "goose" will be so disappointed that she didn't tag "it" (which is essentially impossible, since the goose has to take the time to stand up while the person who is "it" is already off and running) she'll cry and want to stop playing the game entirely.

This is not to say that the game should never be played with three- and four-year-olds. It is, in fact, a great way to introduce young children to games with rules. But these typical behaviors demonstrate how new and challenging a game structure can be for preschoolers.

Almost every group game that exists in the world engages the players in some kind of social interaction, such as conversation. Many games also have some kind of physical or cognitive challenge as well. Playground games, such as Kick the Can or Ghost in the Graveyard, tend to be very physical. Table games, such as board games or card games, tend to have more cognitive challenges. Party games, such as Charades or Musical Chairs, often emphasize social interactions but include a mix of physical and cognitive challenges as well. Some games are really just about killing time, such as games played on long car trips like I Spy or Punch Buggy.

Understanding Chance and Luck

A significant variable in games is the degree of luck or chance. Some games are completely driven by luck, with no skill involved at all. In the board game Hi Ho Cherry-O, for example, each player taps the spinner to find out how many cherries he will gain or lose from his tree. Some games are entirely driven by skill. The board game Rush Hour, in which players strategically move playing pieces shaped like vehicles around a board in order to clear a path for an ice cream truck, leaves nothing to chance. Many games incorporate some combination of luck and skill. In the card game Memory, for example, players must find pairs of cards that match. During the first few turns of the game, when players begin randomly turning over cards, a player may get lucky and find a match. But as the game progresses and some of the cards have been viewed and then turned back over, it takes skill (in this case, a good memory) to be able to find the correct matches. The popular game Battleship is similar. During the early stages of the game, when players begin guessing, pure luck will result in a "hit." But as the game progresses, it is the player who uses an organized strategy, combined with a good memory, who is able to find success.

Very young children, from toddlers through age six or seven, do not yet understand the concept of luck or chance. To understand this concept requires some knowledge of probability, the formal or informal calculation of how likely or unlikely it is that an event will occur. This is a fairly sophisticated mathematical concept. For example, the spinner in the Hi Ho Cherry-O game is divided into six spaces. There is a one-in-six chance that the pointer will land on the bushel basket, which means all your cherries have been spilled. Each game consists of at least six turns per player, so it is probable that each player will get the bushel basket at least once per game. Adults and older children who play the game may not stop to calculate the probability of the bushel basket, but they have a general sense that this outcome may happen to them during the game. A younger child, who does not yet understand even a general sense of probability, chance, or luck, may be very upset if she gets the bushel basket, and wonder if she somehow played the game wrong. Learning these concepts takes time and experience.

> *Very young children, from toddlers through age six or seven, do not yet understand the concept of luck or chance.*

Learning to Lose

Even when children understand a game, learning how to win and lose takes some emotional maturity. Children often take games seriously and want very much to win. Parents often wonder whether they should let their child win a game by giving him some kind of unfair advantage. My experience as a parent and as a teacher is that there's no harm in letting children win games when they are young and still learning, especially between the ages of four and seven, when their cognitive development is progressing quickly but they do not yet have the emotional maturity to handle the frustration of losing. After age seven or eight, however, children should begin to develop some resilience and patience when playing games and dealing with losing. Playing games together as a family is a great way to support children in their growing understanding of how to play by the rules, how to be fair, and how to lose gracefully.

Playground Games

While parents and families play an important role in children's understanding of games, most children also learn a great deal from playing games with other children, on playgrounds, in backyards, during recess, or in school yards. As children get older and have the experience of playing without close adult supervision, they initiate and govern their own games. Parents often look back fondly on the times when they played freely outdoors with other children; the rough, risky, creative, and very exciting play of playground or school yard games. When given the opportunity to initiate and supervise their own games, children often play running-around games like Tag. Playground games have rules, but children will often negotiate or re-create rules, based on the particular landscape where they are playing. A big tree in the center of the playground might become home base, or an area of the blacktop might become "hot lava."

Much of what we know about the history and creativity of children's playground games comes from the research of two British folklorists, Iona Opie and Peter Opie. In the mid-twentieth century, they interviewed children and collected audio recordings of children's games, rhymes, chants, and songs. The Opies published two landmark studies, *The Oxford Dictionary of Nursery Rhymes* (1951) and *The Lore and Language of Schoolchildren* (1959). They found that the most popular playground game among children was some form of chasing game. Whether it was called Tag or Tig or Tig-Tag or Bonkers, the basic game involves someone who is "it" who must chase the other players. Children everywhere seem to enjoy developing variations of Tag, such as Shadow Tag or Freeze Tag, and often heighten the drama of the game by making "it" a zombie or ghost or vampire or robot.

In addition to running games, children enjoy creating and playing other games of physical strength or dexterity, such as thumb wars, arm wrestling, staring contests, jump rope games, or clapping games. The Opies found evidence that these kinds of games have been played by children for hundreds or even thousands of years. (The first documented occurrence of Patty Cakes comes from 1698 [Opie and Opie 1951].) Many rhymes and songs get passed between children for generations, such as this clapping game that is still played today:

> A sailor went to sea, sea, sea
> To see what he could see, see, see
> But all that he could see, see, see
> Was the bottom of the deep blue sea, sea, sea.

When the Opies asked children how they had learned these songs and games, a surprising number of them insisted that they, or other children at their school or in their neighborhood, had made them up themselves. They were unaware that many of the songs and games they played had been around for decades and perhaps even for centuries.

When adults today get nostalgic about the playground games they played with other children when they were young, they often express concerns that children don't play that way anymore, that organized sports have taken over children's free time, and that in many neighborhoods it's not safe for children to play outdoors without supervision. These perceptions are based on reality. It's true that children today play outdoors less frequently than the generation before and that some neighborhoods are not safe for children. The research of the Opies and others like them reassures us that children are resilient and creative and that they will still find ways to play their own games on their own terms. It's also true that parents today may not recognize the versions of playground games that have evolved since they were children. For example, in the past few years many children and teenagers have enjoyed a resurgence in the Cup Game, a game in which children tap and move a plastic cup or cups to create complicated rhythms. The popularity of the Cup Game can be attributed to a scene in the 2012 movie *Pitch Perfect* in which actress Anna Kendrick performs the song "You're Gonna Miss Me When I'm Gone" while accompanying herself with a plastic cup. This sparked many children to imitate Anna Kendrick and create their own games and songs with cups. While many adults might dismiss the prevalence of the Cup Game as just another viral Internet sensation, it's important to note that real children are playing these games with real cups. They are developing dexterity and coordination through repeated practice, and they are having fun using ordinary materials found around the house. While today's games may be inspired by movies, YouTube videos, or other media sources, it's not all that different from the way children passed down rhymes in school yard jump rope sessions a century ago.

Parents today may be concerned about the sexual nature of some of the songs and dances that spread on the Internet, and there are certainly valid reasons for this concern. But we sometimes forget that children have always enjoyed experimenting with "forbidden" topics. Consider jump rope rhymes that have been around for generations:

Lincoln, Lincoln, I been thinking
What the heck have you been drinking?
Looks like beer and tastes like wine
Oh my gosh, it's turpentine!

I love coffee, I love tea,
I love the boys and the boys love me.

Tell your mother to hold her tongue,
She was the same when she was young!
(Hastings 1990)

These patterns of play and the similarities between games over time suggest that children need opportunities to play their own games in their own ways. As mentioned earlier, children need experience taking risks to learn and to develop. When children make up irreverent song lyrics and playground games, they are taking risks with language and poking fun at the world of adults. These play experiences with friends are common among children in many different walks of life.

Board Games

Given that children older than five often prefer peers to parents when it comes to playground and school yard games, especially those related to taboo subjects, parents who still want to play games with their children often turn to table games such as board games or card games. This is an excellent strategy, particularly because many table games, especially board games, are fun for groups of people with mixed abilities and ages. As illustrated by Ellie and Kate's family in their game of Parcheesi, even children who are too young to fully understand the game can still participate, with a little support from the other players. In early childhood education, we call this "scaffolding": parents and family members facilitate and assist the participation of the younger, less knowledgeable, and less skilled children. The developmental psychologist and theorist Lev Vygotsky emphasized the significance of this kind of facilitated learning for young children. According

Many table games, especially board games, are fun for groups of people with mixed abilities and ages.

to Vygotsky, Kate and her parents were serving as the "More Knowledgeable Other" when they helped Ellie participate in the game. Ellie could not have played the game without assistance; the game of Parcheesi was within Ellie's Zone of Proximal Development, the concept Vygotsky created to describe the rich learning that takes place when children's understanding is scaffolded by adults or by other children. The Zone of Proximal Development is the zone between what children can do or know independently and what they are able to accomplish with assistance. When families play board games together, the younger children are not only challenged cognitively by participating in an activity that is complex and advanced, they also experience the emotional satisfaction and confidence that comes from being included and supported by others, in this case by the people they love the most, their parents and siblings.

Board Games and Cognitive Development

The potential benefits of board games for developing children's cognitive and academic skills are immense. At Northwestern University's Center for Talent Development, many of the programs for academically gifted and talented children incorporate the use of board games that challenge students and help to develop their math and analytical skills. As mentioned earlier in this chapter, understanding probability is an essential part of learning to play many games well and developing strategies for success. Many board games develop other math and analytical skills, such as counting, calculating, recognizing patterns, and making predictions. The cognitive benefits of playing board games have been recognized by the American Association of School Librarians, a group that has aligned gaming with twenty-first-century learning standards. Here are just a few of those standards, along with descriptions of how playing games supports them.

Inquire, think critically, and gain knowledge.

1.1.9—Cooperative games require collaboration and information sharing for a team to be successful.

Draw conclusions, make informed decisions, apply knowledge to new situations, and create new knowledge.

2.2.2—In a game, players have to be aware not only of their own actions but also the actions of other players or elements within the game. Players have to be able to think about what others might do and how it will impact them.

2.4.4—Complex, long-term goals in games require constant evaluation of progress and development of new directions for investigation of elements that will lead to the final solution.

(Harris 2014)

Most children seem to aspire naturally to learning new and more complex games. As children progress to more complex games, from Candy Land to Clue or from Checkers to Chess, they develop increasingly more complex strategies. The analytical skills that allow us to think ahead, to troubleshoot, to predict and anticipate problems are highly regarded in the twenty-first-century classroom and work-place. Tech visionary and entrepreneur Bill Gates promotes the game of Bridge as an ideal laboratory for the development of twenty-first-century problem-solving skills, and he has invested significant funds in programs that promote Bridge playing in schools.

These analytical skills are highly regarded in the twenty-first-century classroom and workplace.

Euro-Style Board Games

In Europe, especially in Germany, board games are much more popular than in the United States. Each year, more than 100,000 people attend the annual Internationale Spieltage Essen Spiel, or Essen International Game Days, where game publishers and retailers premiere the latest ideas in board games. In recent years, Americans have become more familiar with Euro-style games through the success of Settlers of Catan, which originated in Germany. Euro-style games, while often a bit more costly than American games, are often beautifully designed. Whereas American games usually have a single victor and, like Stratego or Battleship, have military themes, many Euro-style games allow every player to gain victory points and the themes are often about building community. In Settlers of Catan, for example, players gather resources, build roads, and develop towns. In addition to Settlers of Catan, other Euro-style games that have gained favor in the United States include Carcassonne, Dominion, and Ticket to Ride. For families with older children, ten and up, these games offer an interesting alternative to some of the more familiar American board games.

Beyond Monopoly

During my research on board games, when I talked with adults and children of various ages and stages in life, I was surprised by how often, when I mentioned board games, people would bring up Monopoly. It seems like Monopoly is the "go to" game among American families, or at least the game you see most frequently offered in stores as an example of a family game. I wasn't surprised, however, to hear many people confess that they don't really *like* playing Monopoly. The game is very linear, in that all the players literally follow the same path, and there is very little real strategy to the game, once you understand it well enough to know that you need to buy and develop property in order to collect rent and fees from the other players. The game takes quite a long time to get going and a long time to finish. Most children and even many adults will lose interest before the game actually ends. What does it say about American capitalism when the only real excitement in the game of Monopoly comes from going to jail?

There are so many other, better games to be played. Here is a list of suggestions, loosely organized by children's ages. Keep in mind, as discussed earlier, that children can and often do enjoy participating in games that are well above their playing ability, even though they will require support and assistance during the game. In general, the games progress from the simple to the complex. The more complex the game is, the more opportunities there are for interaction among the players. This list includes a number of Euro-style games in the teen/adult range.

Beginning Board/Table Games (ages 4–5)

Hi Ho Cherry-O

Candy Land

Connect Four

Hungry Hungry Hippos

Don't Break the Ice

Chutes and Ladders

Intermediate Board/Table Games (ages 6–8)

UNO

Battleship

Apples to Apples Junior

Checkers

Trouble

Mancala

Sorry!

Hedbanz

Big-Kid Board/Table Games (ages 9–11)

Ticket to Ride

Pictionary

Clue

Chess

Qwirkle

Name 5

Blink

Blokus

Othello

Teen/Adult Board/Table Games (ages 12 and up)

Dominion

Settlers of Catan

Diplomacy

Backgammon

Bridge

Balderdash

Carcassonne

Scattergories

Game Night!

Several times a year, the families on my block get together for a neighborhood game night. Ages range from as young as two to as old as seventy. We usually start out the evening with easier games for young children, such as UNO or Chutes and Ladders, on the floor or at several tables. Often the highlight of the evening is when the whole group gathers together for a word game or a party game such as Balderdash or Scattergories. One of the pleasures of an intergenerational gathering like this is seeing the teenagers participate and interact with neighbors who are both older and younger. A group game can be a great equalizer, a chance to shed the typical narrow roles that families can fall into. During a game, parents can be silly and awkward and kids can be the bosses who "beat" the adults. Playing a game together fosters connections between friends and family members, between adults and children, and creates memories that last a lifetime.

FINDING AND COLLECTING THINGS

Licking a dripping ice cream cone, five-year-old Caleb sits on a bench next to his older sister, Lauren, at the Beach Freeze snack stand along the shores of upper Lake Michigan. Stopping for ice cream on the last day of vacation is a family tradition. Soon Caleb, Lauren, and their parents will pile into the family's old Subaru and begin the long drive home.

By the time Caleb finishes his cone, drips of melted ice cream have traveled down his right arm, all the way to his elbow. But before he joins his sister along the shore, to wash his hands in the lake water, Caleb stands over the Beach Freeze's overflowing garbage can, rummaging through the discarded cups and napkins.

"Caleb! What are you doing?" his mother cries. "Get away from that mess!"

It's hard to tell whether Caleb is intentionally ignoring his mother or if he really doesn't hear her. He continues rummaging in the trash, focused on his task.

"He needs another blue spoon," Lauren, Caleb's sister, explains to her parents.

Their mother sighs. "Why didn't he just ask me? I had a blue spoon with my sundae."

Lauren shakes her head. "No, that won't work. You had a big blue spoon. Caleb needs a little blue spoon."

"Got it!" shouts Caleb, raising a sticky hand in the air. He is clutching a tiny blue plastic spoon, the kind used at Beach Freeze to offer a small taste of a particular flavor to customers who need help deciding what to choose.

Caleb carries the little blue spoon to the water's edge where he carefully washes it in the water. His mother leans close and helps him rinse his hands and forearms as well. When she is satisfied that he is clean enough for a five-hour car ride, they say good-bye to the lake and Caleb buckles himself into his car seat.

During the long drive home, Caleb plays with the plastic spoons he's collected over the course of the entire summer. He's amassed about twenty spoons and has divided his collection into "families." Some of the spoon families are grouped by color. The new tiny blue spoon joins a family with two larger blue spoons (the parents) and one other small blue spoon, "the sister." Other families Caleb created share similar characteristics. There is a family of four red spoons, all the same size, that have the words "Dairy Barn" molded in raised letters along the handles. One of Caleb's favorite spoons is unique and has no family. This is a special spoon, from the Tastee King, with the shape of a crown at the end of the long handle. Caleb has named this spoon "King Crown" and made it the ruler of all the other spoons.

Caleb's mom occasionally sneaks a peek at her son in the rearview mirror. She smiles. She's grateful he has found a way to amuse himself during the long ride. She shakes her head and shrugs as she wonders, "Who could have predicted that a collection of plastic spoons, salvaged from the rubbish bins of ice cream shops across the Upper Peninsula of Michigan, would provide so much pleasure and intrigue to one little boy?"

Collections and Collecting

The urge to search for treasures, to find, collect, and keep things of value, is likely connected to the basic human instincts for hunting and gathering that humans have shared since people first walked the earth, searching for food or other items that would help them survive. Steven W. Anderson, a neurologist at the University of Iowa, studies brain activity related to hoarding and has identified an area in the prefrontal cortex that appears to control collecting behaviors. Anderson's research has shed some light on both normal and abnormal collecting behaviors and suggests that the desire to acquire and retain objects is nearly universal (University of Iowa 2004).

The collecting behaviors of young children may be tied to a basic human instinct to hunt and gather. Children's first collections, like Caleb's plastic spoons, tend to be items that adults would consider of little value. The first collections of young children are usually items they come across in their immediate environment, things that exist in nature, such as rocks and shells, or manufactured items that would be considered garbage by most adults, such as plastic spoons and bottle caps. Adults may purchase and give children collectible items, such as dolls or figurines or snow globes, but the collections that children initiate and manage themselves are the most meaningful to them and tell us the most about their interests and ideas.

The motivation for starting a collection varies from child to child. Often an item will simply catch the eye, such as a rock with flecks of mirrorlike silver. You pick it up and bring it home. A few weeks later, another rock catches your eye, this time a smooth stone. You just like the way it feels in your pocket. And so it begins. Eventually you have enough rocks to begin sorting and organizing them by size and color. This was a similar process for Caleb and his plastic spoons. One day at an ice cream parlor, Caleb became enchanted with the small, flat, plastic spoons given to customers to eat their Italian gelato. Although Caleb prefers ice cream to gelato, he made it a point to order gelato so he could get one of the little flat spoons. Now, each time the family visits any ice cream or gelato parlor, Caleb pays close attention to the color, size, and shape of the plastic spoons. At some point in the process, he began using the word "collection" to describe the spoons he keeps in a plastic box.

For both children and adults, aesthetics often play an important role in collections. We enjoy saving things that are colorful, are beautiful, and give us pleasure to look at. Or we may start collecting items that are related to a passionate interest in a specific topic. For example, a child who is very interested in horses and hopes to own a real horse someday may begin collecting horse figurines. As the collection grows, the child learns more about the different breeds of horses and their characteristics. The same may be true of adult collectors. A musician with a passionate interest in American folk music of the 1950s and 1960s may begin collecting recordings, photographs, and publications from that time period.

Although some adults may be motivated to develop collections for profit in the hopes that someday the items in their collection will increase in value, profit is rarely a motivation for young collectors. A child as young as four or five is not likely to understand that a tattered *Superman* comic book from the 1940s may be worth hundreds or thousands of dollars. Children are more interested in the special meaning the items have in their own lives, in their play, in their imaginations, and in their friendships.

The Role of Friendships in Collecting

Social relationships tend to be a strong motivator for collectors, both children and adults. Friends or family members may be role models who also collect, or the collection becomes something special that can be talked about or admired by others. Children feel important when they have a collection they can show to other people and talk about in great detail. In a study of elementary school children and their collecting behaviors, researchers Stacey Menzel Baker and James W. Gentry found that many children were motivated to begin collections because they saw their friends collecting and they wanted to be part of that group. For example, a fifth grader reported, "Well, one of my best friends started collecting. He had some really neat rocks so I thought if I could get some neat rocks like him" (Baker and Gentry 1996). Other motives for collecting that were reported by the children in this study included an escape from boredom or from reality, an opportunity to learn more about a special topic, and a passion for specific objects. Along with the desire to connect with friends, an almost opposite reason was also expressed as a motivation to collect things: the desire to be different from other people, to demonstrate to the world through your collection that you were special and unique. For example, a child might choose to collect something odd or unusual such as dog toys or toothbrushes.

Regardless of the original motivation for starting a collection, one of the more universal pleasures of collecting is the opportunity to sort, organize, and display the array of items collected. Collecting things allows children to create order and control in a world where they are still rather powerless. The desire and impulse to control and organize loom large in the psychology of collecting. Both children and adults often use mathematical concepts to sort and categorize the items in their collections. The concept of *seriation*, for example, may be used in a doll collection, when a child lines up the dolls from smallest to largest. Or a collection may be sorted into categories by various attributes, such as sorting coins by color (gold, silver, copper). Other children, especially young children like Caleb in our opening scenario, may organize their collection into "families" or create a story or narrative to tell about the personality of each item. Baker and Gentry's study found that many children take great pleasure in the organizing and maintenance of their special collections. For example, a first grader named Brayha who was interviewed for the study described her rock collection: "Every day when I get them I like [to] wash them and then I put them on my dresser and then when they get dirty I wash them again" (Baker and Gentry 1996).

> Collecting things allows children to create order and control in a world where they are still rather powerless.

Our collections are an expression of who we are; they are part of our identity. Psychoanalyst Werner Muensterberger asserted that we desire certain objects because they represent our personality. Our collections reflect our interests and preferences, and the decisions we make as we organize and expand our collections may even demonstrate unspoken wishes and emotions, such as the desire to control or contain a world that can sometimes seem chaotic and overwhelming (Muensterberger 1994). This perspective was echoed by the experience of Andrew Ackerman, executive director of the Children's Museum of Manhattan, which hosted an exhibition of children's collections called *Great Stuff.* Ackerman noted that for children, collecting "becomes an exercise in creating a world all their own, a world they have control over" (Stevens 1998).

Many children experience a sense of comfort in creating, organizing, and tending to their collections. This may be especially true of children and adults who, for whatever reason, sometimes feel more comfortable with objects than with people. Children who have experienced a loss or a stressful experience may particularly benefit from becoming collectors. Searching for, discovering, and saving special objects gives a child a sense of control over her environment that she may find soothing and reassuring. Moreover, a child who has trouble socializing or communicating with other children may treat his collection like a group of friends, personifying the objects much like Caleb, the child in our opening scenario who created "families" out of his plastic spoon collection. Based on my experience working with young children, I've observed that starting a collection often provides children with a positive, constructive coping strategy in response to stress or loneliness.

A passionate interest in a particular topic, such as sharks, soccer, geology, or fashion design, may motivate children to collect. For example, Baker and Gentry interviewed a fifth-grade girl who collected plastic and glass horses. She said, "I find information about horses in like catalogs, magazines, and stores when we go there. I can remember like, look at a horse and remember when I got it and who gave it to me, stuff like that. I've read that book [her best friend had given her *The Love of Horses*] about ten times already. I like to go to the library and check out books on how to keep horses and train them. I spend a lot of time thinking about horses, I mean really like them, I want to be a horse trainer when I grow up" (Baker and Gentry 1996). As demonstrated in this example, many children engage in pretty intense research and study as part of the development of their collections. They become highly motivated to learn, read, and discover more about the subject of their collections. For some children, the process of collecting things related to their topic of interest may even lead to an avenue of academic study or a career choice later in life. Mihaly Csikszentmihalyi, the author of *The Meaning of Things* (1981), has written about the potential for personal growth in childhood collections. He states that children "may grow out of the collection, but it will have a lasting effect. . . . For instance, the child who collects butterflies and one day becomes a naturalist" (Stevens 1998).

Twenty-first-century children seem to be less interested in collecting than their parents and grandparents were when they were children. Many scholars and researchers, such as game expert Irving Finkel, argue that the general trend toward the commercialization of childhood and of play has led to a diminishing interest in collecting. Finkel stated in a BBC interview, "What's really exciting about collecting is looking for things that you can't find when you want them. All you need to find [mass market collectibles] is the money. The real thrill is lost" (BBC Radio 4 2003). When all it takes to create a collection is a credit card and an Internet connection, it's easy to understand why the pleasure of searching and discovering has diminished.

Very young children, however, who are picking up plastic spoons, rocks, or other items found on the ground, are less aware of this trend toward commercialization. The commercialization becomes more an issue when children get a bit older, around first grade, when they start to become aware of themselves as consumers. If we wish to recapture the innocent pleasures of collecting for the pure joy of it, we can look back in time at children in the early twentieth century and see what they enjoyed collecting. In 1906, Chicago schoolteacher Elizabeth Howe conducted a survey of middle school students to see what they collected and why they enjoyed the activity. Her purpose was to show that children's collections give teachers and parents a window into children's lives: "It is quite clear that the teacher who had such information would have an insight into the children's inner life which she would hardly be able to get in any other way" (Howe 1906, 467).

Many of the items children collected in 1906 are similar to the items collected today, such as coins or dolls. Some of the items are more surprising. Several of the children Howe described collected things that simply don't exist now, such as calling cards. Other children collected things that seem to have very little value, such as broken cups and saucers. One child collected rags, and one child reported collecting birds' wings. Another collected "turfs from Ireland." The reasons the children gave for collecting were very similar to children's explanations today. Some reported that collecting was a social activity; their friends were collecting things, so they wanted to do it, too. Howe reported that many children seemed to be more interested in quantity than quality. She writes that some of the children simply "wanted to see how many they could get" (Howe 1906, 467–68). Today, amassing a large collection of items that can be purchased, such as baseball cards or Japanese erasers, does not involve skill, knowledge, or social connections to the extent focused collecting did a hundred years ago. Often increasing the size of the collection just requires the right amount of money.

Regardless of the impact commercialization and our consumer culture have had on young people, there are still many children who enjoy collecting today. Here is a curious but not comprehensive list of things children enjoy collecting, divided into relevant categories.

Things from Nature

rocks	skulls
gems	seashells
minerals	pieces of coral
fossils	sand
butterflies	leaves
insects	flowers (dried or pressed in a book)
cicada shells	seeds
snake skins	pinecones
nests	nuts
eggs	gourds
bones	hives

Found Items

bottle caps

tabs from soft drink cans

twist ties

spoons

toothpicks

swizzle sticks

straws

string

rubber bands

empty spools

empty matchboxes

lint

buttons

Popsicle sticks

pieces of foil

candy wrappers

condiment packets

sea glass

jars

Cards

baseball cards

playing cards

commercial trading cards
   (such as Pokémon cards)

greeting cards

valentines

business cards

old gift cards

key cards

Toys

Matchbox cars

model cars

Tonka cars

teddy bears

dolls

rubber ducks

Lego minifigures

Littlest Pet Shop animals

trolls

games

game pieces

action figures

animal figures

nesting dolls

puppets

toys related to a specific character
   from a book, movie, or TV show,
   such as *Star Wars* or *Harry Potter*

Things Related to a Celebrity (movie star, musician, athlete)
photographs
autographs
bobblehead dolls

Souvenirs

snow globes
thimbles
postcards
refrigerator magnets
salt and pepper shakers

patches
plates or ashtrays or shot glasses
bottle openers
flattened pennies

Household Items

nuts and bolts
wire
rusted things
doorknobs
keys
locks
key chains
lanyards

Indian brassware
lunch boxes
mouse pads
candles
flashlights
pencil sharpeners
erasers

Holiday/Religious Items

Christmas ornaments
menorahs
Halloween masks

Curiosities

miniature things
giant things
fortunes from fortune cookies
typos (printed things with mistakes)

Print or Paper Items

journals

stamps

stickers

books

comic books

pens

pencils

envelopes

signs

paper dolls

paper snowflakes

tickets

Items Related to a Hobby or Interest

toe shoes

musical instruments

hockey pucks

Items of Value

coins

paper money

jewelry

pins

antiques of any kind

Clothing or Accessories

T-shirts

bow ties

hair clips

baseball caps

flip-flops

coin purses

scarves

mittens

Intangibles

jokes

coincidences

smells

While many collectors, both adults and children, may describe themselves as "serious" collectors, let's remember that collecting is, at its heart, a kind of play. From the search for special items to the sorting and organizing of the collection, the process of collecting brings excitement and joy to children's lives. At the beach in summer, one young child will shout to another, "Let's look for shells!" and the hunt begins. Pretending, or fantasy play, is often a significant element in collecting, especially when children name the objects they collect, organize them into families, or create stories about them.

When it is truly child-centered, there is a free and playful quality to all aspects of the collecting process. "Child centered" means that the child initiates the collecting activity, chooses what to collect, and makes independent decisions about what to collect, where to look, and how to store and organize the collection. Parents can certainly play an important role in children's collections, but ideally the child is in the driver's seat.

A parent's first job is recognizing (or remembering, from her own experience) the common childhood desire to collect; the thrill of searching for, finding, and keeping things that a child feels are valuable or interesting. Collecting is an activity that usually takes place at home, not at school, so parents are in a unique position to play an important role in supporting and facilitating their children's collecting activities. The research on the value of collecting in children's lives also emphasizes the importance of the parent's role in children's collecting. In the study described earlier, Baker and Gentry concluded that children benefit when parents play a facilitating role in collecting, especially at the crucial point when children first enter into the collecting process. "Parents were mentioned more than three times as

> *"Child centered" means that the child initiates the collecting activity and chooses what to collect.*

frequently as friends and siblings . . . in discussions of how the collections were started. Most mentions were of gifts which started the collection or of continuing additions on birthdays and other holidays" (Baker and Gentry 1996). Even when children had easy access to the things they wanted to collect, such as items found in nature, they often mentioned the important role of their parents. For example, one of the children in the Baker and Gentry study noted the role his father played in developing his collection. "When I was little, my dad would always pick up rocks and I would look under them and pick up the bugs underneath them" (Baker and Gentry 1996).

Knowing that very young children will demonstrate their first impulse to collect by picking up items in their immediate environment, parents are in a unique position to either encourage or discourage the collecting behavior. When a two- or three-year-old picks up a stick or a stone or a bottle cap at the park and wants to keep it, the parent can respond warmly to the child's action, acknowledging the child's curiosity and desire to hold and keep the object, even if bringing the item home is not a safe or practical choice. Suppose, for example, your child finds an empty vodka bottle at the park, the miniature kind that contains just one or two shots. It's easy to understand why a child might find the size and the shape of the bottle unique and fascinating. On the other hand, most parents would agree that a discarded vodka bottle is not a safe or appropriate plaything for a small child. We can both educate our children about the hazards of these items and acknowledge the children's healthy curiosity and observational skills ("What an interesting bottle. It's very small, isn't it? But we shouldn't touch it because it might be dirty or broken, and that wouldn't be safe").

As children grow older, we can help them develop their own critical thinking skills by modeling safe collecting habits and offering simple, age-appropriate explanations for why some items are okay to pick up and keep and other items are not. This same discernment process applies to natural items as well as to garbage. For example, a papery chunk of an old wasp nest, long abandoned by any live creatures and found on the sidewalk beneath the eaves of a garage, would be safe to bring home, while an active wasp nest hanging from a tree with wasps flying around it would certainly not be safe to acquire, even for the most avid young naturalist.

Observe your child and see what topics and items capture his or her interest, then support that interest. Collecting can be a hobby a parent and child enjoy together, a special time they spend together. Parents can help in the search for items or help with the storage or organization of the items. For example, a child who has started a collection of buttons might simply store them in a jar, or perhaps the child might enjoy attaching the buttons to a display board. A parent's help would be needed with the gluing or sewing involved in creating the display. When parents help create a place of honor for a collection, a special shelf or drawer, a mini museum in the child's bedroom or the family room, children feel affirmed and valued for their development of the collection.

Parents can also help children access information that will enrich the collecting experience. A child who has collected abandoned nests or bits of eggshells or feathers would probably enjoy using a pair of binoculars to observe the birds in the neighborhood. A reference book, such as an illustrated bird guide, might also help deepen the child's interest and spark new ideas for developing and expanding this young naturalist's collection.

If your child begins collecting items that must be purchased rather than found, the process of shopping for these items can also be a special experience that you share together. For example, a child who collects baseball cards might enjoy visiting a baseball card shop or a collectors' conference, or going to garage sales or flea markets where these items are for sale. Shopping for collectors' items can certainly be accomplished online, but visiting stores or sales, seeing the actual items on display, and touching them yields a much richer experience, especially for children. The Internet can also be a valuable source of information for collectors. For example, the website for the Smithsonian museums in Washington, DC, includes an interactive section for children who are interested in starting a collection. See Smithsonian Kids at: www.smithsonianeducation.org/students /idealabs/smithsonian_kids.html and click on "Amazing Collections."

Let Your Child Take the Lead

Not every child will be interested in collecting. And some young children may begin a collection with great enthusiasm, only to switch to a different collection or abandon the process entirely when something new captures their attention and imagination. But as children get older, their attention span will naturally expand and many will find great pleasure in collecting the items that intrigue and entertain them. When this happens, you will be ready to enjoy it with them.

Telling Stories with Toys

*Five-year-old Paige plays with toys on the floor, under the dining table,
while her older brother, Andrew, seated at the table, draws pictures with
colored pencils and markers.*

"Help! Help!" calls Paige, holding a small yellow toy. "I'm getting captured!"
*Paige plays with several plastic ponies, each with a beautiful mane and tail. The
yellow pony in her hand has colorful butterfly stickers scattered across its flanks,
like equine tattoos.*

"I can save you!" *A pink pony has come to the rescue of the yellow one. Paige
holds one pony in each hand and makes them run across the floor, between the
table legs.*

"Look out! Look out! The witch is coming . . . Oh no, now we're both getting
captured . . . Quick, quick, make the magic potion . . . Here's some chemicals and
beakers and the powdered formula . . ." *Paige moves the toys around the floor,
making the ponies scamper around.*

"Poof! Poof! Bam! It worked, we're invisible!" *Paige holds both ponies up in
the air.* "No one can ever see us again." *Paige crawls out from under the table, still
holding the ponies. She looks over her brother's shoulder and watches him draw.*

"Is that Spider-Man?" *asks Paige.*

"Yep," *nods Andrew.*

"Can you make the ponies?" *Paige sets her toys on the table.*

Andrew shrugs.

"Make Spider-Man and the ponies," *suggests Paige.* "They can go to a planet
together."

"Spider-Man already went to Saturn, see?" *Andrew points to a large orb with
rings that he drew earlier.*

"Hmm." Paige studies Andrew's drawing. "The ponies were there, too."

Andrew sighs. "No, they weren't. There aren't any ponies on Saturn."

"They were!" says Paige. "But you can't see them because they're invisible!"

Satisfied, Paige crawls back under the table. Andrew gets back to work on drawing Spider-Man.

Toys as Characters in Children's Pretend Stories

Playing with toys is certainly common behavior among children. While some toys, like puzzles or board games, are intended to be used in a specific way, toys such as dolls, action figures, or plastic animals can be held, manipulated, and arranged in an endless variety of scenarios. Toys that represent people, animals, superheroes, villains—all variations of human beings and creatures—are the stars in the dramas that children imagine as they play. Each time a child manipulates this type of toy, she is telling a story, with conversation and actions, but also sometimes almost entirely in her head. Telling stories with toys is an essential play experience because it is another form of pretend play, an extension of the dramatic play described earlier. While the golden age of dress-up-style pretending takes place when children are preschool age, usually three to five years old, the pretending that takes place when children manipulate and tell stories with small toys, the way Paige plays with her ponies, is a form of play that can begin when children are very young, around three, and continue for many, many years, through grade school, often until ages twelve or thirteen.

Growth and Development through Play

Telling stories with toys is an activity that both demonstrates and supports children's cognitive and language development. The leap from pretending with your own body, such as putting on a cape and becoming Superman, and pretending with objects, such as action figures, that are not part of your own body is a milestone that demonstrates a child is able to think with greater abstraction and sophistication. Generally, all growth in cognitive and language development is a progression from the simple to the complex, from the concrete to the abstract, and from the real to the imagined. Consider how children learn to count and calculate. First they use their own bodies, such as counting on their fingers. Then they are able to use objects and items, such as pennies or an abacus, to count. They are moving from a tactile, sensory, and kinesthetic understanding to an understanding that is demonstrated and practiced externally.

By manipulating objects, the way Paige manipulates the ponies under the dining table, a child is able to create a narrative that is much bigger and more complex than what she could act out with her own body. For example, the story Paige created and told with her toys had to do with two ponies and a witch. Paige held a pony in each hand and summoned the image of the witch in the words she used as she played. It's important to note that many children, like Paige in this scenario, talk out loud as they play, even if they are playing alone. Paige created a story in which her ponies were in grave danger and they resourcefully rescued themselves by creating a magic potion that made them invisible, but she developed the story, with a suspenseful plot and exciting action, for her own satisfaction and entertainment, not to please or entertain anyone else.

Masters of an Imaginary World

Children are usually not even aware that they are creating stories when they play and pretend. If you asked a child, "What story are you creating right now?," he would probably look at you incredulously and say, "I'm just playing." But through the observations and studies of child psychologists, early childhood educators, and other researchers, we have evidence that children's pretend fantasies include many of the same elements of great fiction or theater. For example, the acclaimed Tools of the Mind early childhood program in Denver, inspired by the work of Russian psychologist Lev Vygotsky and developed by educators Elena Bedrova and Deborah Leong, is based on the idea that pretend play is a core experience in child development (Tough 2009). Bedrova and Leong advise parents about the transition from dress-up pretending to playing with toys, emphasizing the similarities between the stories children create and a sophisticated theater production:

> Children will begin to play more with little dolls and action figures instead of dressing up and playing the roles themselves. They may engage in "director's play," in which they talk and act for the figures, playing several roles and changing their voices for each of the actors. Things can get pretty complicated with a long period of discussion of who is doing what and when, followed by the acting out of the scene that was just planned. Lego toy sets (with people) and dollhouses encourage this kind of play. Children will want to own a theme set, which helps in acting out certain scenarios, but you should also encourage them to add pieces from other sets to promote their creativity and flexibility. (Tools of the Mind 2014)

The complexity and variety of the stories children create with toys demonstrate a significant leap in children's cognitive and intellectual development. As children get older, their stories become increasingly more complex in the level of detail, in the use of dialogue and the depth of characterization, and in the sophistication of themes and problems the characters encounter.

Social-Emotional Development

Telling stories with toys is a richly satisfying play experience for children that also supports and reflects their social and emotional development. Jerome Bruner, notable educational psychologist and author of *Acts of Meaning* (1990) and *The Culture of Education* (1996), has observed that narrative, or stories, are a basic and primary way in which human beings organize their world. In his books, Bruner describes how children have a natural bent toward a narrative organization that emerges at an early age. While Bruner has asserted that children's richest learning experiences come from narrative, I would assert that the richest *play* experiences also come from narrative. The creation of stories, as a free and spontaneous play experience, helps children express, reflect upon, and understand their world and helps them to connect to others through the social interactions that take place during play.

Children's play narratives, such as the story Paige created with her ponies, have been studied by child development researchers. Jiryung Ahn and Margot Filipenko, for example, observed that there are three universal themes or categories in children's play narratives: narratives about the self, narratives about other people, and narratives about the broader world (2007). The first category, self, includes pretend scenarios in which the child represents herself or her identity in play. The second universal theme, other people, is demonstrated through stories in which children explore their relationships with other people, such as friends and family. The third theme, which is the most sophisticated and abstract, includes narratives in which children explore abstract scientific or philosophical issues, such as stories about animals or stories that depict a battle between good and evil. The research confirms what many parents and teachers already know intuitively, from watching children play: by creating pretend narratives with toys, children learn and express who they are, how they relate to other people, and how they understand their world.

Toys for Sale

Even parents who well understand the valuable role of toys in their children's growth and development may become confused and disheartened when shopping for them. The huge quantity and variety of toys on the market is overwhelming. For me, as a parent and an educator, I find that a focus on the idea of *story* helps me to evaluate which toys are going to best inspire

> *Selecting a toy for purchase is like casting an actor in a film.*

and support children's play. When we are selecting and purchasing toys for our children, we become the casting directors in the films our children are creating. With this in mind, we can organize toys into several general categories.

Realistic People Toys

The term "doll" usually refers to a fairly large toy, such as a life-size or near-life-size baby doll that children can hold and cradle in their arms like a real baby. Another common size for a doll is the eighteen-inch child doll, such as the popular American Girl dolls. This size doll works well for children who enjoy playing with doll clothes and accessories. An eighteen-inch doll is large enough for small hands to manipulate the clothing, shoes, and other accessories, but still small enough that children can move them around during the creation and dramatization of their imagined stories.

Toy figures that are realistically proportioned but smaller, usually from about four to six inches tall, are often sold as dollhouse accessories. Many children enjoy playing with small people figures even if they don't have a dollhouse to put them in. Some realistic people figures are also available as components in larger toy sets or branded toy systems, such as the Playmobil line of toys. Dolls and people toys are rarely completely realistic in their features, skin color, and proportions. Instead of hands, for example, Playmobil figures have notched slots designed to hold other toys and props from the Playmobil system.

Fantasy People Toys

Here I'm using the term "fantasy people" to refer to toy figures and dolls, such as the classic Barbie, that have been designed deliberately to differ from a realistic human form. This includes "action figures," such as super-heroes, that are represented as having magical powers, as well as figures that blend human and technological features, such as Transformers.

In addition to the classic Barbie dolls, this category includes a variety of "fashion dolls," such as Polly Pockets, Bratz dolls, or Monster High dolls. This also includes the wide variety of Disney princess dolls and other toys based on licensed media characters.

Realistic Animal Toys

Like real human beings, actual animals with realistic features are fairly underrepresented in the toy market. Stuffed animals take on a variety of forms and styles, some more realistic than others. Children tend to use larger stuffed animals for comfort and cuddling, but smaller animals, such as Beanie Babies, are easier for children to manipulate when they are creating imaginary stories. Many children enjoy playing with small plastic or resin animal figures fashioned in realistic shapes and colors, such as the line of animal toys sold by the German toy company Schleich.

Fantasy Animal Toys

Paige, from our openings scenario, plays with toy ponies that fall into this category. The proportions, colors, and design of these animals are not realistic. Often they are based on mass media characters or television shows. Examples include toys with brand names such as My Little Pony, Hello Kitty, Calico Critters, or Littlest Pet Shop. Fantasy animal toys sometimes represent magical creatures, such as dragons or unicorns, or animals with special powers or human characteristics, such as Furbies or Pokémon figures.

Random Stuff Kids Find or Get

Many of the toys American children currently encounter in their daily lives are the trinkets that are given to children as prizes or treats or included in other purchases as promotional items. A common example is the McDonald's Happy Meal toy. Party favors such as plastic spiders or little toy trolls, the small inexpensive doodads that children receive at birthday parties, are another example in this category.

Do-It-Yourself Toys

Many children play with toys that are made by hand, not manufactured, such as cloth dolls or puppets sewn by friends or family members or purchased at craft fairs. Some children enjoy making their own toys and figures out of cloth or clay or other craft materials, or they make toys with found objects such as sticks and rocks.

Commercialism and Gender Roles

A recent visit to the toy aisle in my neighborhood big-box store revealed ample evidence of the lack of diversity in the current toy market. I found an aisle of predominantly pink toys, such as princess dolls and collectible animal figures, and an aisle of predominantly black and blue toys, such as action figures and robots. The toys were grouped together by brand and each package prominently displayed the brand's logo and slogans.

The majority of toys available seem to fall into the categories of fantasy people and fantasy animals. It's difficult to find toys that realistically represent people and animals. Based on the packaging and presentation of the toys, it's also really clear which toys are marketed to girls and which to boys. For example, toys for boys are packaged in dark colors, mostly blue and black along with some bright red, and the design features of boys' toys, such as oversized motors and rockets, seem to promote the value of power and violence. Toys for girls are packaged in pink and other pastel colors, and the features of these toys, such as long, flowing hair on both humans and animals, seem to promote attractiveness as the most important characteristic. The gender segregation of toys has been the subject of study for sociologists and educators, as well as the focus of attention in the media. The concern voiced among parents and pundits is that the gender biases represented in toys are teaching girls to value, at best, helpfulness and physical appearance and, at worst, sexuality and submission, while toys are teaching boys to value, at best, strength and action and, at worst, violence. Organizations such as the Campaign for a Commercial Free Childhood (CCFE) (www.commercialfreechildhood.org) identify and publish information for families warning against toys that promote gender stereotypes, such as the

Dallas Cowboys Cheerleader Barbie Doll, which won CCFC's "Worst Toy of the Year" award in 2009.

Activism for toys that challenge gender stereotypes recently received a boost when a start-up toy company, GoldieBlox, created several web and TV advertisements that depict little girls rebelling against the tyranny of pink playthings. The tide may be turning. Some major retailers are starting to listen to parents' concerns about gender bias in the design and marketing of toys, at least in the United Kingdom, where a grassroots parent-led campaign called "Let Toys Be Toys" has gained traction. London department store Harrods and British supermarket chain Morrisons both recently made the decision to phase out the dividing of toy displays into the two distinct categories of boys' toys and girls' toys (Davies 2014).

One of the grounding concepts at the heart of this book is the idea of balance. The parenting pendulum need not swing all the way in one direction or the other. All things in moderation. You must draw the line in the sand for your family wherever you see fit, but know that it won't damage your little girl's self-esteem if she plays with a pink toy. And your little boy won't grow up to be a violent criminal if he plays with an action figure. The important idea is that children should have the freedom to create stories on the three levels described earlier—self, others, and the world. They can best do that when they are exposed to a wide variety of materials, toys, and experiences and are allowed, through their play, the opportunity to make their own mark on the world. Rudolf Steiner, the philosopher who inspired Waldorf schools, emphasized the role of the imagination in children's development. In Waldorf classrooms, children play with beautiful yet plain cloth and wooden toys. The idea is to give children a blank slate on which to develop their own fantasies and ideas. Even if a family does not subscribe to a Waldorf approach to education, this general idea that children benefit from at least some experience playing with unadorned, open-ended materials seems like a wise and helpful perspective.

The idea is to give children a blank slate on which to develop their own fantasies and ideas.

Many children also enjoy creating stories on paper, such as Paige's brother, Andrew, drawing Spider-Man pictures while his sister plays under the table with her horses. Drawing is another way that children play, by telling stories with their drawings, weaving a narrative around the layers of marks on the page. For many children, from the time they develop the dexterity and small-motor skills that allow them to create representational drawings, often around five years old, drawing becomes an important part of their daily lives, a play experience that is much more focused on the process of creating a story than on the work of art that is the result or product of their play. Some children talk as they draw, in very similar ways that children talk as they play with toys, describing the action and narrating the dialogue of the characters. Listening to children's stories as they draw can be a great pleasure for parents, teachers, and caregivers.

> *Some children talk as they draw, describing actions and narrating dialogue of their characters.*

Jon and Charlie, eight-year-old friends, are drawing together at the kitchen table in Jon's home. Jon's mom offers them colored markers, but the boys prefer drawing with plain number 2 pencils.

Jon begins drawing right away, but Charlie just watches.

"That a pirate ship?" he asks.

"Nope," says Jon. "Not yet."

"Gonna be?" asks Charlie.

"Maybe," says Jon. "Haven't made the pirates yet."

Charlie, inspired, starts drawing. "I'm making some pirates."

The two boys draw in silence for several minutes. They look only at their own pages, absorbed and concentrating.

"Arrgh!" exclaims Charlie.

"What?" asks Jon.

"The pirates are taking over this ship." Charlie points to his picture. Jon nods and smiles with appreciation.

"Me, too," says Jon. "The pirates are coming, but the ship is speeding up. They might get away."

"Boom! Boom!" Charlie quickly draws long, sweeping lines across his page. "Cannonball!"

Jon laughs and follows Charlie's lead. "Cannonball!" Jon draws long lines, ending in a dark circle, the cannonball traveling through the air.

"Bull's-eye!" shouts Charlie.

"Crash!" shouts Jon. "The mast is broken. They're taking in water!"

"Ahh!" screams Charlie, poking holes in his paper. "We're sinking!"

Jon smiles as he watches Charlie destroy his drawing. Then he returns to his own page, drawing lines across the flat side of his ship. He announces, "My guys patched the leak. Got away."

Charlie nods and grabs a fresh sheet of paper. "Look out for those mermaids. They've got poison candy . . ."

The conversation between Jon and Charlie as they draw is indistinguishable from the conversation they might have if they were playing with toys. They play with the images they are drawing on the page the same way they would manipulate toy figures. Each created his own narrative about a ship attacked by pirates. Although Jon's story ended differently from Charlie's, the boys still influenced each other, collaborating in the development of their unique and separate plot lines. For example, Charlie was inspired by Jon's idea to draw a ship, and Jon was influenced by Charlie's cannonball battle to add the same excitement to his story. The pleasure of this experience was not in the creation of a finished drawing, a work of art, but in creating and telling the stories.

Jon and Charlie's drawing experience demonstrates researcher Susan Wright's description of the significant meaning of children's drawing process:

In children's drawing, for example, the assembled signs can include graphically produced images (e.g., people, objects), which might also include written letters or words, numbers, symbols (e.g., flags) and graphic devices (e.g., "whoosh" lines behind a car). In addition, this graphic content may be accompanied by children's sounds (e.g., expressive vocalisation) and imitative gestures to enhance the meaning. Hence, when children draw, they construct and interpret a range of verbal and nonverbal signs with reference to the conventions associated with this medium of communication. (Wright 2007, 37)

Wright posits that when children create stories by drawing and talking, they function as film directors creating a movie. Even though the children are not using cameras and may not have any experience with how cinematography works, they pay attention to the same narrative and cinematic devices that film directors use to tell a story—such as sequencing, close-ups, sound effects, and building action. Wright likens the drawing process to "roleplay on paper" (Wright 2007). Although not every child enjoys the drawing process and using it to create narratives, for those who do, drawing pictures is often their favorite form of play.

Parents and Children Playing Together, Side by Side

For parents who want to spend time playing with their children by engaging in the telling of stories, on paper or with toys, the challenge is figuring out how, as an adult, to join the play without directing or interrupting the child's creative process. This can be difficult, especially for parents who are eager to express their own creativity. Case in point: In the fall of 2013, many social networking websites and Internet trend watchers took note of a family celebrating "Dinovember" by sharing Instagram-style photos that the parents had posted capturing their children's toy dinosaurs in various funny poses. The dad, Refe Tuma, posted the photos and a commentary on http://Medium .com: "Every year, my wife and I devote the month of November to convincing our children that, while they sleep, their plastic dinosaur figures come to life. It began modestly enough. The kids woke up to discover that the dinosaurs had gotten into a box of cereal and made a mess on the kitchen table."

The Internet was charmed and amused by the funny photos of toy dinosaurs posed as if caught in the act making all kinds of mischief: writing on the walls with crayons, breaking a vase, wrapping themselves up in toilet paper, and so on. Many of the parents who commented online expressed both admiration as well as a sense of discouragement in their own parenting skills ("You're so creative. I wish I was a fun parent like you!"). The children of the Dinovember parents were certainly very fortunate to enjoy the delightful surprises of these funny dinosaur dioramas. But we "ordinary" parents must remember that our primary job as parents is not to entertain our children but to support their growth and development. There's a time and place for each of the different functions of parenting—for guidance, feeding, caregiving, teaching, and, yes, entertaining. But when our children are creating their own stories, through play with toys or drawing, or whatever form of pretending and fantasy play develops, our role as parents is to get out of the way and let their magic happen. When I suggest that parents "get out of the way," I'm not saying to leave the room. I propose parents play side by side with their children, literally and figuratively, when their children engage in this kind of fantasy play. Share the fun, listen and ask questions, maybe even crack a few jokes—but try not to lead.

Homes, Hats, and Habitats

Important supporting roles for parents to take in telling stories with toys include prop master, scenery builder, and costumer. Adults have resources and skills that children are still developing—they can help hunt down a cardboard box just the right size to make a castle, they can use a hot glue gun to attach sticks together in the construction of a miniature tree house, they can stitch together fabric to make a doll's bridal veil. These are some very tangible ways parents can help support children's pretend play with toys while still letting the children follow their own vision for the path of their stories. Parents can also support children's pretend play with toys by documenting the stories the children are creating. Many children really enjoy having their parents take photos, make audio or video recordings, or write down dialogue or plot summaries that record the drama the children create with toys and props.

Rich Source Material

Another important role parents play in children's storytelling and imaginative play is making sure their children have a rich variety of source materials to draw from, both real-life experiences and good literature. Taking children on trips and outings, meeting interesting people from all walks of life, and visiting zoos and museums are just a few examples of the variety of life experiences that influence children's imaginative play. Reading stories from many different traditions and cultures also helps expand children's horizons and feed their creativity.

Reading stories from many different traditions and cultures also helps expand children's horizons and feed their creativity.

Many parents know that visiting their local public library is a great way to help their children develop a love of reading and great literature. But not every parent knows where to find folktales and fairy tales in the children's section. Did you know that classic fairy tales like *The Three Billy Goats Gruff* or folktales like *The Firebird* are actually shelved among the nonfiction books, not the picture books? In the Dewey decimal system, books related to folklore are designated as 398 and folk literature is grouped under 398.2. Folktales and fairy tales make great source material for children who enjoy incorporating magic in their pretend scenarios. When children see that there's more than one way to tell the same story, they will be freer and more creative in their imaginative play. You can help expand your children's creativity and imaginations by visiting the 398.2 books in your library, where you will find multiple presentations of the same folktale or fairy tale from the perspectives of different authors and illustrators. This is an important lesson to learn, especially for children who are excessively enraptured with toys based on mass media characters; they need to know that it's okay to play stories that are different from what they see on television or in video games. For example, the Disney versions of fairy tales, such as *The Little Mermaid, Beauty and the Beast,* and *Sleeping Beauty,* have become iconic in American culture. Many children are both surprised and intrigued to discover that other authors and artists have told these same stories in many different ways across a diversity of cultures.

When you visit the 398.2 books in your library, you may also want to help your child explore some of the lesser known folktales and fairy tales that have not been as overexposed in mass media entertainment. Here are some suggestions of stories that have been told and illustrated by many different authors and artists, yet have potential broad appeal among both boys and girls:

The Ant and the Grasshopper
The Boy Who Cried Wolf
The Firebird
The Gingerbread Man
The Golden Goose
Hansel and Gretel
The Little Match Girl
The Little Red Hen
Peter and the Wolf
Rumpelstiltskin
The Steadfast Tin Soldier
Strega Nona
The Three Billy Goats Gruff
The Six Swans

Jerome Bruner wrote in *The Culture of Education,* "We simply do not know, nor will we ever, whether we learn about narrative from life or life from narrative: probably both" (Bruner 1996, 94). In the context of children's play with toys, I take this statement to also mean that children's play is shaped both by life experience and by the written, spoken, and dramatized narratives that are presented to them as stories through books, movies, theater productions, and oral storytelling. There is a fluid and organic nature to stories played and interpreted by our children. As parents, we are privileged to be invited to sit in the front row for these performances.

Making Things Happen with Machines

Cold rain mixed with ice taps against the living room window as Sydney, age seven, and her little sister, Ruth, age four, arrange half a dozen couch cushions in a circle on the floor. They're building a fort while their mom works on her laptop nearby in the dining room. She's trying to file her taxes, so she's relieved that the children have found a way to amuse themselves on this gloomy Saturday afternoon.

"Mommy, can we use a sheet?" Sydney asks. "It's for a roof."

"Sure, honey," replies her mom. "You can get a sheet out of the linen closet."

A few minutes later, Sydney is back. "Mommy, can we use this box?" She has pulled a large cardboard box out of the recycling bin.

"Sure, honey," replies her mom.

"And this tube?" Sydney holds up a paper towel tube. "And some tape?"

"Yes, yes, that's fine," says her mom without looking up from her computer screen. "Take whatever you need."

A good forty-five minutes passes before Sydney returns and invites her mother to come and visit the completed fort. Their mom has been so absorbed in her calculations and tax forms that she doesn't even realize so much time has passed.

"I'd love to see your fort," she replies, closing her laptop.

In the living room, four-year-old Ruth's voice can be heard, singing, from inside the fort, a circle of cushions and chairs covered with a big bed sheet.

"Hi, Mommy!" Ruth peeks out from inside the fort.

"Hi, sweetie!" her mom replies.

"Look, we made a drawbridge!" Sydney shows her mom how they flattened the cardboard box into a flat door, then attached it to the end of a long jump rope using tape. The other end of the rope is threaded through a paper towel tube and the tube is taped to one of the chairs that holds up the sheet.

"I'll show you how it works," volunteers Sydney. She pulls on the end of the jump rope that has been threaded through the tube. The rope tugs on the door and the door lifts and hangs, a bit crooked, covering the entrance of the fort.

"And when we want to let people in, we can lower the drawbridge like this." Sydney slowly loosens the tension on the jump rope until the cardboard door lies flat on the floor.

"Wow," says their mom admiringly. "That's really cool."

"Want to come in, Mommy?" asks Ruth.

"That's, okay, sweetie," her mom replies. "I think I'm too big."

"No," protests Ruth. "It's big in here. Plus I want to show you the window I made."

"Okay," her mom says. "I'll come see your window."

Ruth and Sydney's mom gets down on her hands and knees and crawls over the drawbridge, into the fort, followed by Sydney. The cloth roof sags in the middle, but there's plenty of room for the three of them to sit together on the floor.

"Here's the window I made," says Ruth, pointing.

"Wait, what's my iPad doing in here?" asks their mom, surprised.

"That's the window, Mommy," replies Ruth.

"You're using my iPad for a window?" her mom asks. Ruth nods, and her smile disappears. "Ruth, honey, Mommy's iPad is really expensive. You can make a window out of something else."

"No, Mommy, look out the window," Ruth presses the home button on the frame of the iPad, refreshing the image on the screen. Her mom immediately recognizes the photo—it's a picture she took from their hotel window when their family was on a summer vacation along the Pacific Ocean. The water is bright blue and the sun is shining warmly.

"See, Mommy," says Ruth. "Our fort has a nice view of the water."

For a moment, their mom is speechless. The image from their vacation has taken her back to that happy time and she is overcome with longing for that carefree beach, the warmth of that sun, the happy laughter of her children as they dug in the sand. Then she looks at the smiling faces of her children, here in this fort on this cold rainy day, and realizes that they have built a time machine, a place that re-creates the pleasure of living along that sandy shore. While she was busy doing her taxes, her children were busy visiting the coast of Oregon and constructing a *vacation home with a working drawbridge that opens to welcome their favorite visitors.*

"I love that window," she says to Ruth. "And I love this whole fort." She reaches over to put her arms around her children and accidentally tugs the roof a little, creating a gap between it and the walls. "Oops, sorry!"

"That's okay, Mommy," Sydney says. "We know how to fix it."

Don't Be Afraid, It's Only Technology

When parents express apprehension about the role of technology in the lives of their children, they're usually referring to electronic devices with screens, such as laptop computers or tablets, electronic game systems, cell phones, and televisions. It can be reassuring to parents to take a step back and look carefully at how these electronic devices fit into the entire diversity of useful machines created by human beings that make our lives richer, easier, and safer than ever before. I use the term "machines" here instead of "technology" because children incorporate all kinds of machines into their play, including simple nonmotorized toys that move, such as yo-yos and spinning tops, as well as machines and toys with basic motors powered by a variety of sources, such as windup toys and battery-powered toys. Sydney, for example, in the construction of her fort, created a very simple machine, a pulley, to operate her drawbridge.

In the field of physical science, the term "simple machines" refers to devices that have no internal source of energy. There are six classical types of simple machines:

- the lever
- the wheel and axle
- the pulley
- the inclined plane
- the wedge
- the screw

Most complex machines, devices that are powered by an external energy source such as electricity, incorporate one or more of these simple machines. Many children's toys incorporate the mechanisms of a simple machine. A toddler's pull toy, such as a duck on a string that waddles as the child tugs it along, incorporates the wheel and axle as well as the lever, which moves up and down to make the duck waddle. While most children don't formally study simple machines and physical science until middle school and high school, children learn a great deal about how machines work through their play and the manipulation of toys. They learn to predict the motion of an object, they explore the effects of the movement of one object on another object, and they discover ways to change the speed or direction of an object. Imagine a child playing with a toy car, rolling it across the floor or the surface of a table.

> Children learn a great deal about how machines work through the manipulation of toys.

Almost anything the child does with that car, such as letting it roll off the end of the table and crash to the floor, helps the child better understand how the world works. Playing with toys that move, with motorized toys, and with electronic toys and devices gives children experience with the entire broad continuum of concepts and functions that make up what we call "technology."

Children enjoy making things move or make noises or light up (for example, by pushing the buttons in the elevator). Children enjoy using machines and technology in play because they like to make things happen and they like to imitate the people they admire, such as their parents and older siblings and pretty much anyone with a cell phone. Even small toddlers are enchanted by play experiences that demonstrate cause and effect. You shake a bell and it rings. You push a toy truck and it rolls across the floor. You drop a marble in the top of a marble maze tube and it rolls all the way to the bottom. Children, like adults, are also attracted to novelty; they enjoy seeing and trying new things, so they are drawn to the screens of computers and tablets and cell phones like moths to a flame. Most children also begin to get the message, at a very young age, that cell phones and computers are important in the lives of adults. They begin to equate electronic devices with power.

Simple to Complex

As described in previous chapters, children's cognitive development progresses from the simple to the complex, from the concrete to the abstract. So children's play that involves machines will develop from tactile and kinesthetic experiences, such as shaking a rattle to make a sound, to complex and abstract interactions, such as playing with an iPad or tablet. If they make this shift too quickly or too exclusively, without a broad variety of experiences in between, children miss out on the opportunity to build a foundation of understanding for how things work.

There's nothing wrong with children using electronic games and devices, and, in fact, there are many benefits that will be explored later in the chapter, but these experiences must be balanced with other kinds of involvement with machines that represent a range of mechanisms and many different levels of complexity. It's important for children to learn, through play, how the magic is made The significance of direct experience with how things work is expressed by David Elkind in his book *The Power of Play: Learning What Comes Naturally*: "The complexity of electronic technology changes the child's intellectual engagement with these toys. The mechanics of soapbox cars and windup toys are easy for children to understand. Toys with embedded microcontrollers, in contrast, work as if by magic. . . . It is at least possible that children's inability to figure out how their playthings work can dampen their scientific curiosity"

> *It's important for children to learn, through play, how the magic is made.*

(Elkind 2007, 23). Fortunately, children can learn a great deal about technology through their direct experiences with toys.

Developing an Understanding of Technology

Many of the ordinary toys that children use in play can be sorted into three categories that represent increasingly complex layers of technology:

- simple machines
- machines with motors
- computers and other electronic devices

Among the toys that operate as simple machines, there is a great variety of notable playthings. In fact, the esteemed Victoria and Albert Museum of Childhood in London, which houses a vast collection of childhood-related objects from the 1600s to today, has created an interactive display of "moving toys" that demonstrates the range of play experiences that fuel children's understanding of machines, mechanisms, technology, and how things work. The museum's Moving Toys Gallery is divided into four sections: "Pushes and Pulls," "Springs and Cogs," "Circuits and Motors," and an eclectic collection of optical toys titled "Look See." You don't have to visit the museum to understand the variety of mechanical and technological concepts at work in children's toys. These categories will likely sound familiar to you and inspire memories of your own childhood toys.

Pushes and Pulls

Toys that children push or pull are simple machines in that they have no internal sources of power. The force that causes them to move comes from the movement of the child's body or from the force of gravity. Examples include pull toys such as a duck on a string with wheels that waddles when the child pulls it along. Other toys pulled by strings include yo-yos and marionettes. Toys powered by the force of gravity include all kinds of different rolling toys and balls, such as marbles that follow the path of least resistance along a tube or gutter that makes up a "marble run." Another external force that causes toys to move is air, generated either by a human being blowing with the mouth, such as balloons and balloon boats, or by the natural movement of air by wind, which powers toy sailboats and toy paratroopers.

Springs and Cogs

Toys with springs and cogs are also simple machines that are powered by an external energy force such as friction or the winding of a spring. Children can race toy cars, trucks, or trains that are powered by friction by spinning the rear wheel backward, winding up the friction wheel, and then allowing the vehicle to speed ahead when the energy is released. A similar mechanism is at work in toys such as jack-in-the-boxes that contain a spring coil. The spring is compressed and then let go, releasing energy as the toy bounces up and down. Windup toys can be small or large and represent all kinds of animals, people, and vehicles.

Circuits and Motors

Toys with circuits and motors may include some elements of simple machines such as wheels and axles, but they are more complex because they are powered by an internal source, a flow of electricity, or by energy stored in a battery. For example, many train sets run on electricity. Toys that operate by remote control, often with a handheld console, are powered by motors. Toy vehicles are not the only playthings powered by circuits and motors. Many dolls and stuffed animals are designed to move or make sounds through the use of motors. Motorized toys usually perform only one or two simple actions at a time, such as a doll that moves her head and makes a sound.

Look See

A kaleidoscope is a toy, usually shaped like a cylinder, that allows the child to view changes in color and light when the toy or parts of the toy are moved or rotated. A basic kaleidoscope has no internal source of power and uses only the light available externally. Yet the pleasures of viewing a kaleidoscope are remarkably similar to the pleasures of viewing a computer screen. We are fascinated by the movement and changes of light. Examples of other optical toys that project or manipulate light include view-masters and toy cameras. Computer games and electronic devices with screens are more sophisticated and contemporary examples of optical toys, yet they all belong on the same continuum from the simple to the complex.

Twenty-First-Century Play Experiences

Comparing a simple spinning top, powered by a child's hand, to electronic video game systems, such as Xbox or PlayStation, seems like a giant leap, yet all these are part of the same toy family. The technology of twenty-first-century computer games, whether accessed through a specific game system or using smartphone apps, did not fall into our laps by magic. It is the result of steady human progress and innovation over many centuries of research and experimentation.

Children who are born and growing up in the twenty-first century will be part of an increasingly complex world with rapid and continuous innovations in new technology. Getting along in this world will require a certain level of comfort and skill with using technology. We want our children to function successfully—to be able to adjust a thermostat, make a phone call, drive a car, and so on. Most children want that, too, and are eager to learn about the world. They want to use technology in their play experiences because they enjoy feeling powerful and accomplished.

There may also be educational value in playing computer games, especially for learning STEM subjects (science, technology, engineering, and math). New research indicates that the use of computer games in classrooms may have a positive impact on academic achievement (Shapiro et al. 2014). Play experiences that involve technology may not only be fun and satisfying, they may also provide educational advantages.

Coding for Beginners

Children who are fascinated by electronic devices and computer games may enjoy learning about computer programming, or "coding." Educational apps like Daisy the Dinosaur or Kodable teach basic coding concepts to children as young as four years old. Scratch, a free and accessible programming language developed by MIT Media Lab, was recently adapted for use by young children in a free app called Scratch Jr. The simple "drag and drop" block programming in Scratch Jr. allows children to create their own animated stories and games. The website code.org is another terrific source for parents, educators, and children to learn more about computer science. I recommend that parents of children ages five and above complete one of the online "Hour of Code" tutorials with their child. You may be surprised by how fun and easy coding can be, and your child may be inspired to undertake more complex programming challenges in the future.

Tech Parenting

Guiding our children to make smart and safe choices regarding the use of technology can be challenging when there are so many choices of devices, systems, apps, and programs. Parents often feel intimidated by the complexity of new technology, and we fear that if our children's knowledge and expertise advances beyond our own, we might become incapable of providing supervision and guidance.

The concept of balance and moderation can be useful here. A common goal among parents is to make informed and intentional choices about the role of technology in our families and in the lives of our children.

Parents do need to set reasonable and appropriate limits on screen time, the amount of time each day that children spend looking at screens and engaging with technological devices. Sometimes the hardest part for parents is modeling these limits. We need to practice what we preach and set aside our own devices from time to time. We also need to commit time to

A common goal among parents is to make informed and intentional choices about the role of technology in our families.

sitting with our children and exploring games, apps, systems, and machines together so that we share knowledge and vocabulary. Parents are not in this alone. There are many excellent resources and organizations to help families make these kinds of decisions together.

One example is Common Sense Media (www.commonsensemedia.org), a nonprofit organization whose mission is to "empower parents, teachers, and policymakers by providing unbiased information, trusted advice, and innovative tools to help them harness the power of media and technology as a positive force in all kids' lives." One of the primary functions of Common Sense Media is providing information to parents about various products such as electronic games and phone apps as well as movie reviews to help them make decisions about what entertainment and play experiences are appropriate for their children.

Another great source of information for parents is the Fred Rogers Center for Early Learning and Children's Media, named for the beloved star of the children's television show *Mister Rogers' Neighborhood*. In 2012, the Fred Rogers Center published "Advice for Parents of Young Children in the Digital Age." Regarding children's play experiences, I particularly like this advice: "Have fun, stay engaged. Children's media and technology are best when they support active, hands-on, creative and authentic engagement with the people and world around them. Look for games, websites and apps that encourage outdoor activity, healthy eating, critical thinking and other real-world skills."

How Things Work

As children grow and learn, their appetite for more sophisticated technology will naturally increase. Keep children connected to the idea that computers and electronic devices are machines made by people. Fuel children's curiosity about how things are made and how they work. One fun way to do this is to allow children to take their toys apart, especially the "baby toys" that they are no longer interested in playing with. Children will need adult supervision and assistance for these experiments. Compared to other household items, toys can be especially difficult to take apart because they are manufactured to protect children from small, moving parts. Other household machines and appliances, such as toasters and rotary clocks, may be easier to work with. Again, supervision is necessary to ensure that children are not exposed to sharp edges or harsh chemicals.

Opportunities to explore how things work will naturally present themselves in the life of a family. Stuff breaks. Dishwashers leak, pipes freeze, lamps need rewiring. Include children in the discussion and problem-solving process. Next time you buy an item that requires assembly, perhaps a shelving unit, invite your child to assist you as you follow the instructions and figure out how to put it together. And don't be afraid to make mistakes in front of your child. Solving problems and brainstorming solutions when things don't go well can be even more educational (and sometimes entertaining) than when everything goes as planned.

Digital Storytelling, Digital Play

Many of the play experiences discussed in this book involve stories and storytelling. As we've discussed, many educators and psychologists (for example, Jerome Bruner) assert that stories are the primary structure children and perhaps all human beings use to organize and understand their experiences in the world and their sense of who they are—their identity. Keeping in mind the amazing power of narrative in children's play, I see incredible potential in children's use of technology to support their enjoyment of stories, both the receiving of stories from others and the creation of their own stories. Very young children, even infants, can now safely manipulate devices such as cameras, cell phones, and computer tablets. At a very young age, children are able to take pictures, make audio and video recordings,

> *I see incredible potential in children's use of technology to support their enjoyment of stories.*

draw with their fingers on a touchscreen, and animate their own cartoons. Children have the potential to create and tell stories in ways that adults may not even recognize as storytelling.

Giving your child a role as the creator or digital archivist of family stories may be just what you need to calm your fears about technology taking over your family. Take control. Open your laptop and create a folder for your child to store the photos that he takes on your cell phone. Download an app that will let your child record his voice. Breathe. Play. Repeat.

You'll know your child's play experiences are well balanced between playing with machines and technology and other kinds of play when you see a give-and-take, a back-and-forth influence, between these different kinds of play experiences. For example, when a child's active pretend play is based on the characters she viewed in the online video she watched last night. Or when her block structure is inspired by a session of playing Toca Builder or Minecraft on your iPad. Or when she catalogs her button collection using digital photography. Or when she creates a stop-motion animated short starring her favorite stuffed bear. Cross-pollination between play experiences, from analog to digital and back again, reassures us that children are still making important and meaningful connections between their experiences with technology and the heart of their real lives.

Children are still making important and meaningful connections between their experiences with technology and the heart of their real lives.

References

Ahn, Jiryung and Margot Filipenko. 2007. "Narrative, Imaginary Play, Art, and Self: Intersecting Worlds." *Early Childhood Education Journal* 34 (4): 279–289.

American Academy of Pediatrics. Accessed 2014. "Transitional Objects." HealthyChildren.org. www.healthychildren.org/English/ages-stages/baby /pages/Transitional-Objects.aspx.

Anderson, Lorin W., and David R. Krathwohl, eds. 2001. *A Taxonomy for Learning, Teaching, and Assessing: A Revision of Bloom's Taxonomy of Educational Objectives.* New York: Longman.

Baker, Stacey Menzel, and James W. Gentry. 1996. "Kids as Collectors: A Phenomenological Study of First and Fifth Graders." *Advances in Consumer Research* 23, 132–37. Provo, UT: Association for Consumer Research. www.acrwebsite.org/search/view-conference-proceedings.aspx?Id=7928.

BBC Radio 4. 2003. "Why Don't Children Collect Things Anymore?" *Woman's Hour.*

Bos, Bev. 1978. *Don't Move the Muffin Tins: A Hands-Off Guide to Art for the Young Child.* Carmichael, Calif.: Burton Gallery.

Brazelton, T. Berry, and Joshua D. Sparrow. 2001. *Touchpoints Three to Six: Your Child's Emotional and Behavioral Development.* Cambridge, MA: Da Capo Press.

Bruner, Jerome. *Acts of Meaning.* 1990. Cambridge, MA: Harvard University Press.

———. 1996. *The Culture of Education.* Cambridge, MA: Harvard University Press.

Burdette, Hillary L., and Robert C. Whitaker. 2005. "Resurrecting Free Play in Young Children: Looking Beyond Fitness and Fatness to Attention, Affiliation, and Affect." *Journal of the American Medical Association,* January. http://archpedi .jamanetwork.com/article.aspx?articleid=485902.

Burnett, James H. 2013. "Rhode Island's Debbie Sterling Focuses on Creating a Toy for Young Girls to Build On." *Boston Globe,* January 9.

Clements, Rhonda. 2004. "An Investigation of the Status of Outdoor Play." *Contemporary Issues in Early Childhood* 5 (1): 68–80. http://www.allianceforchild hood.org.uk/uploads/media/7_Clements_CIEC_5_1_web.pdf2.pdf.

Common Sense Media. Accessed 2014. www.commonsensemedia.org/about-us /our-mission.

Csikszentmihalyi, Mihaly. 1981. *The Meaning of Things.* Cambridge: Cambridge University Press.

Davies, Katie. 2014. "Morrisons to 'Phase Out Pink and Blue' Toys after Pressure from Tyneside MP." ChronicleLive, February 26. www.chroniclelive.co.uk/news /north-east-news/morrisons-phase-out-pink-blue-6746604.

Elkind, David. 2007. *The Power of Play: Learning What Comes Naturally*. Cambridge, MA: Da Capo Press.

Fred Rogers Center for Early Learning and Children's Media. 2012. "Advice for Parents of Young Children in the Digital Age," April. www.fredrogerscenter .org/resources/early-learning-environment.

Fraiberg, Selma H. 2008. *The Magic Years*. New York: Scribner.

Gopnik, Adam. 2002. "Bumping into Mr. Ravioli." *New Yorker*, September 30. www.newyorker.com/archive/2002/09/30/020930fa_fact_gopnik.

Guggenheim Foundation. Accessed 2014. "The Architecture of the Solomon R. Guggenheim Foundation." *Arts Curriculum Online*. www.guggenheim.org /new-york/education/school-educator-programs/teacher-resources/arts -curriculum-online?view=item&catid=730&id=119&tmpl=component&print=1.

Harris, Christopher. Accessed 2014. "Gaming Alignment: Standards for the 21st-Century Learner." American Association of School Librarians. http://aasl .ala.org/aaslstandindtf/images/4/43/GamingCurriculumAlignment.pdf.

Hastings, Scott E. 1990. *Miss Mary Mac All Dressed in Black: Tongue Twisters, Jump Rope Rhymes and Other Children's Lore from New England*. Little Rock, AK: August House Publishers.

Henkes, Kevin. 1993. *Owen*. New York: Greenwillow Books.

Hirsch, Elizabeth S., ed. 1996. *The Block Book*. Washington, DC: National Association for the Education of Young Children.

Howe, Elizabeth. 1906. "Can the Collecting Instinct Be Utilized in Teaching?" *The Elementary School Teacher*. Chicago: University of Chicago Press.

Johnson, Harriet Merrill. 1966. *The Art of Block Building*. New York: Bank Street College.

Kemple, Kristen M., Jacqueline J. Batey, and Lynn C. Hartle. 2004. "Music Play: Creating Centers for Musical Play and Exploration." *Young Children*, July. Washington, DC: National Association for the Education of Young Children.

Klass, Perri. 2013. "A Firm Grasp on Comfort." *New York Times*, March 11. http ://well.blogs.nytimes.com/2013/03/11/a-firm-grasp-on-comfort/?_r=0.

Kozlovsky, Roy. 2008. "Adventure Playgrounds and Postwar Reconstruction." In *Designing Modern Childhoods: History, Space, and the Material Culture of Children*, edited by Marta Gutman and Ning de Coninck-Smith, 171–190. New Brunswick, NJ: Rutgers University Press.

Krauss, Ruth. 1952. *A Hole Is to Dig: A First Book of First Definitions*. New York: Harper Collins.

Larson, Elizabeth Foy. 2012. "Benefits of Free Range Parenting." *Family Circle*, July. www.familycircle.com/teen/parenting/discipline/benefits-of-free -range-parenting.

Louv, Richard. 2012. *The Nature Principle: Reconnecting with Life in a Virtual Age*. Chapel Hill, NC: Algonquin Books.

Luscombe, Belinda. 2013. "Let Them Throw Cake: Messy Kids May
Be Faster Learners." *Time: Health & Family*, December 2. http://healthland
.time.com/2013/12/02/let-them-throw-cake-messy-kids-may-be-faster
-learners.

McGhee, Paul E. 1971. "Cognitive Development and Children's Comprehension of
Humor." *Child Development* 42 (1): 123–38.

McLeod, Sue A. 2010. "Concrete Operational Stage." *Simply Psychology*.
www.simplypsychology.org/concrete-operational.html.

Medical News Today. 2004. "Newborns Laugh in their Sleep Say Japanese
Researchers," April 18. www.medicalnewstoday.com/releases/7365.php.

Miller, Edward, and Joan Almon. 2009. *Crisis in the Kindergarten: Why Children
Need to Play in School*. College Park, MD: Alliance for Childhood.

Muensterberger, Werner. 1994. *Collecting: An Unruly Passion; Psychological
Perspectives*. New York: Mariner Books.

National Public Radio. 2013. "Dr. Brazelton on Guiding Parents and Learning to
Listen," June 16. www.npr.org/2013/06/16/191695052/dr-brazelton
-on-guiding-parents-and-learning-to-listen.

Opie, Iona A., and Peter Opie. 1951. *The Oxford Dictionary of Nursery Rhymes*.
Oxford: Clarendon Press.

———. 1959. *The Lore and Language of Schoolchildren*. Oxford: Clarendon Press.

Paley, Vivian Gussin. 2004. *A Child's Work: The Importance of Fantasy Play*. Chicago:
University of Chicago Press.

PBS Kids. Accessed 2014. "Fannee Doolee." *Zoom*. http://pbskids.org/zoom
/fromyou/fanneedoolee.

Play England. 2009. "Developing an Adventure Playground: The Essential
Elements," April. www.playengland.org.uk/media/112552/pathfinder-adventure
-playground-briefing.pdf.

Ramirez, Ainissa. 2013. "Making Friends with Failure." *Edutopia*, August 26.
www.edutopia.org/blog/learning-from-failure-ainissa-ramirez.

Rubin, Jeanne S. 1989. "The Froebel-Wright Connection: A New Perspective."
Journal of the Society of Architectural Historians 48 (1): 24–37.

Sears, William. Accessed 2014. "Ask Dr. Sears: Security Blanket." *Parenting*.
www.parenting.com/article/ask-dr-sears-security-blanket.

Selly, Patty Born. 2014. *Connecting Animals and Children in Early Childhood*.
St. Paul, MN: Redleaf Press.

Shapiro, Jordan, et al. 2014. "What the Research Says about Gaming and
Screen Time." *Mind/Shift: Guide to Digital Games and Learning*. New York:
KQED & Games and Learning Publishing Council. www.kqed.org/assets
/pdf/news/MindShift-GuidetoDigitalGamesandLearning.pdf.

Singer, Dorothy G., and Jerome L. Singer. 1990. *The House of Make-Believe:
Play and the Developing Imagination*. Cambridge, MA: Harvard
University Press.

Skenazy, Lenore. 2010. *Free Range Kids: How to Raise Safe, Self-Reliant Children
(Without Going Nuts with Worry)*. San Francisco, CA: Jossey-Bass.

Smith, Laura. 2014. "Outdoor Learning: Education's Next Revolution?" Salon.com, February 16. http://www.salon.com/2014/02/16/outdoor_learning_educations_next_revolution/.

Stevens, Kimberly. 1998. "Children Who Collect a World of Their Own." *New York Times*, November 26.

Taylor, Marjorie. 1999. *Imaginary Companions and the Children Who Create Them.* New York: Oxford University Press.

Tierney, John. 2011. "Can a Playground Be Too Safe?" *New York Times*, July 18. www.nytimes.com/2011/07/19/science/19tierney.html.

Tools of the Mind. Accessed 2014. "Make Believe Play at Home." www.toolsofthemind.org/parents/make-believe-play.

Tough, Paul. 2009. "Can the Right Kinds of Play Teach Self-Control?" *New York Times*, September 27.

University of Iowa. 2004. "Brain Region Identified That Controls Collecting Behavior." *University of Iowa News Services.* http://news-releases.uiowa.edu/2004/december/121504brain.html.

University of North Carolina at Greensboro. Accessed 2014. "Toddlers: Thinking and Learning; Benefits of Messy Play." http://center.serve.org/ss/toddlersmessy-pf.php.

Wells, Rosemary. 1999. *Noisy Nora.* New York: Viking.

Wiederholt, Kristin. 2006. " 'Adventure Playground' a Dying Breed in the U.S." *National Public Radio News*, March 9. www.npr.org/templates/story/story.php?storyId=5254026.

Willems, Mo. 2004. *Knuffle Bunny: A Cautionary Tale.* New York: Hyperion.

Wilson, Ruth A. 2012. "Teaching Among the Trees." *American Forests*, Winter 2012. www.americanforests.org/magazine/article/teaching-among-the-trees.

Winnicott, Donald W. 1953. "Transitional Objects and Transitional Phenomena: A Study of the First Not-Me Possession." *International Journal of Psycho-Analysis* 34, part 2, 89–97.

Winslow, Marjorie. 1961. *Mudpies and Other Recipes: A Cookbook for Dolls.* New York: Macmillan.

Wright, Susan. 2007. "Young Children's Meaning-Making through Drawing and 'Telling': Analogies to Filmic Textual Features." *Australian Journal of Early Childhood* 32 (4): 37–48.